NATURAL TABLES

NATURAL

CHRONICLE BOOKS

San Francisco

TABLES

Nature-Inspired Tablescapes for Memorable Gatherings

SHELLIE POMEROY

Photographs by Corbin Gurkin

Library of Congress Cataloging-in-Publication Data

Names: Pomeroy, Shellie, author. | Gurkin, Corbin, photographer.
Title: Natural tables : nature-inspired tablescapes for memorable gatherings / Shellie Pomeroy ; photographs by Corbin Gurkin.
Description: San Francisco : Chronicle Books, [2022]
Identifiers: LCCN 2021038939 | ISBN 9781797210162 (hardcover)
Subjects: LCSH: Table setting and decoration. | Nature craft. | Entertaining.
Classification: LCC TX879 .P59 2022 | DDC 642/.8--dc23
LC record available at https://lccn.loc.gov/2021038939

Manufactured in China.

Photography by Corbin Gurkin and Shellie Pomeroy.
Styling by Shellie Pomeroy.
Design by Lizzie Vaughan.
Typeset in Caslon and Graphik.

Harper's Bazaar is a registered trademark of Hearst Communications, Inc.; Maytag Cheese is a registered trademark of MDF Food, LLC; Roquefort is a registered trademark of Confederation Generale Des Producteurs De Lait De Brebis Et Des Industriels De Roquefort Association; Silk & Willow is a registered trademark of Mystudiodesigns, Inc.; Stilton is a registered trademark of Stilton Cheese Makers' Association; Tulipina is a registered trademark of Tulipina Corporation; Weck is a registered trademark of J. Weck Gmbh & Co.; X-Acto is a registered trademark of Sanford, L.P.

10 9 8 7 6 5 4 3 2

Chronicle books and gifts are available at special quantity discounts to corporations, professional associations, literacy programs, and other organizations. For details and discount information, please contact our premiums department at corporatesales@chroniclebooks.com or at 1-800-759-0190.

Chronicle Books LLC
680 Second Street
San Francisco, California 94107
www.chroniclebooks.com

To Michael,
my guardian angel.

CONTENTS

Introduction 11   Setting a Natural Table 15   How to Use This Book 35

TABLE DESIGNS

Weekend Brunch
39

Modern Dutch Master
53

Botanical Birthday
69

Date Night In
79

Ocean Inspired
89

Garden Gathering
101

Fun and Fanciful
113

Celestial Celebration
125

Afternoon Tea
137

Plant Oasis
149

Harvest Palette
161

Grazing Table
171

Stocked and Styled Bar Cart
183

Nordic Winter
193

Breakfast in Bed
205

Resources 216

Project Templates 218

Acknowledgments 221

INTRODUCTION

Connecting with Nature

My connection to nature began in childhood. My memory is steeped in the magic of nature's seasonal gifts, which I eagerly anticipated. With spring came purple lilacs and getting lost in the overgrown bushes that lined my neighbor's fence. Summer found me plucking through my aunt Johanne's vegetable garden, with pops of red tomatoes peeking through the abundance of earthy greens and trailing vines. Fall, marked by the changing russet and crimson hues of tree foliage, was closely followed by winter layering a blanket of white against the evergreen trees.

When I was a child, there always seemed to be a special gathering happening, as both my parents came from large, connected families; my dad was one of eight siblings, and my mom boasts fifty first cousins! My cherished childhood memories include birthday parties in the backyard that smelled of freshly mowed grass, summer reunions spent exploring the outdoors at my great-uncle's cottage on the lake, a Thanksgiving table that stretched the length of the house, and walking knee-deep in the snow along the line of cars leading to the Christmas party at my great-aunt's house. It's the elements of nature, from each occasion, that capture these events forever in my mind.

My passion for nature deepened when I started my own family. Determined to pass a love of nature to my daughters, Catherine and Elizabeth, we spent their younger years finding our entertainment and inspiration in our outdoor surroundings. As my daughters grew older, gardening, baking, plant dyeing, knitting, sewing, and crafting with natural materials became frequent activities we enjoyed. Gatherings and special occasions became an opportunity to showcase our creations. Homemade beeswax candles, hand-carved wooden bowls, and pinch-pot ceramic vases are just a few of our handcrafted pieces. It's incredible how these simple items, combined with a few flowers or branches clipped from the yard, transformed our table. Before any party or event, my first stop for design inspiration was just outside my door. No matter the season, there always was and still is a bounty of decor waiting to be gathered.

My business, Silk & Willow, emerged following years of exploring nature and studying its beauty. In my work as a textile artist, I have created naturally dyed textiles to adorn tables in grand museums, in castles, in villas, at celebrity affairs, and at intimate gatherings at home. Through all these, I have one universal thread that addresses diverse styles and client expectations: the love of natural elements—natural color, textures, and layering these elements in a natural, organic way.

My botanically dyed, relaxed, soft, gauzy textiles offer an alternative to the typical stiff, synthetic, and one-size-fits-all pressed table linens. The foundation of each of my table designs, these naturally dyed linens create a warm and inviting atmosphere. This book will share resources, tips, and some easy recipes that I hope will encourage you to start crafting your own collection of botanically dyed textiles at home.

If you're like me, you don't have one design aesthetic that defines you. Bohemian, minimalist modern, eclectic, and moody design styles all appeal to me. My table designs range from pure and simple to overflowing with details. The one constant is the underlying thread of utilizing natural elements to create a welcoming presentation. Nature is perfectly imperfect. Setting your "natural table" is not about perfection; instead, knowing a few time-honored principles will allow

you to create with ease and flexibility when setting your table. Beneath the surface of all great art and design is a set of rules used to make the work appear effortlessly balanced and beautiful. The same is true for your tablescape design.

There's a universal connection we all share with nature. Natural colors, textures, and materials have a way of appealing to our senses while providing an endless source of beauty. We resonate with the hues crafted from flowers, roots, and branches because our eye perceives this living color as nature—soothing, inviting, and familiar. This book is a celebration of nature, and an invitation to incorporate natural elements into table presentations to add beauty, warmth, and harmony to your gatherings.

Whether you're planning an intimate meal or are hosting a more significant milestone, your table will be a focal point and set the stage for the nourishing meal to come. With *Natural Tables* as your guide, my hope is that you have fun harvesting natural materials, scouting thrift and antique stores, getting dirty in the garden, playing in the kitchen, and staining your hands in dye pots! Let nature be your inspiration for designing a unique tablescape to make any occasion feel extra special.

SETTING A NATURAL TABLE

Inspired by Nature

Like any other design discipline, tablescape design should be functional and serve a purpose, be aesthetically pleasing, and tell a story. To accomplish this, balance, repetition, scale, contrast, and harmony are among the principles that can be used to guide you when setting your table. A degree in design isn't necessary to apply these theories; we all have an intuitive understanding of these values from what we've observed and learned through nature. With all of its interacting parts, nature constantly provides us with an abundance of examples and inspiration for applying these principles. When we observe the mountaintops against the open sky, the markings on a butterfly, a waterfall, moss on a rock, or a field of wildflowers, we are experiencing perfect design. Learn from what you see and carry it into your tablescape design.

Natural Color

Color has the power to elevate our mood and awaken our spirit. Before the advent of synthetic dye in 1856, textile color was derived from natural sources: different parts of plants, animals, and minerals. These organic sources create complex colors that cannot be replicated in synthetic form. Seeing color, not from a swatch book, but pulled, literally, from the landscape and memorialized into fabrics is a way to bring nature, in a lasting form, into your tablescape design. Colors from nature can be bold and intense or soft and subtle. Natural colors have a warm and inviting allure that resonates with the onlooker. Aware or not, we all share a universal connection when we view natural colors; we receive these colors as if experiencing nature itself.

Texture

Textures layered on your table can create illusions of space, depth, and movement. Much like a walk along a path or through a woodland area, the textures we encounter have the power to grab our attention and draw us into the experience: the curling bark on a tree, a velvety flower petal, or the smooth surface of a rock. Similarly, textures on your table create visual interest and guide the onlooker through your tablescape design. We long to touch and experience textures, making it a wonderful way to engage your guests.

Foraging Design Elements

Nature is a free source of beauty. Flowering weeds on a roadside, plants that have gone to seed, fallen pods, branches, leaves, vines, and grasses are just a few of the natural elements you can forage and incorporate into your table design. Before you forage, here are a few guidelines: Always get permission to forage on private property or follow your city guidelines, tread lightly without disrupting the landscape, seek out invasive species, take only what you will use, limit yourself to 10 percent or less of what's available, use clippers, and do not pull the roots to ensure regrowth.

My gardens and access to acres of land for foraging provide me with a bounty of natural elements throughout the season. Whether I use fresh clippings or gather and dry flowers and branches for future use, I'm always harvesting natural elements in various textures and colors to incorporate into my table designs. Get creative! Some of the most unlikely elements can create a wow factor when incorporated into your tablescape design.

A set of linens, dinnerware, glassware, flatware, a few timeless accessories, and nature are the foundation of your styling elements. Classic and versatile pieces will help you conserve storage space and allow you to mix and match for larger gatherings. I have been collecting tableware and accessories for years, and some of my first pieces are still favorites I use daily. Classic pieces can be adapted to any theme and can be accessorized or embellished with charger plates, napkins, name cards, menus, or botanicals for fancier occasions.

Linens

A collection of linens in an assortment of sizes, textures, and colors is essential to creating a variety of different tablescape designs. Even when using the same dinnerware and flatware, an array of styled tablescapes can be created by incorporating table linens. The drape, color, and texture of your linens change the look and mood of your table. Choose heavier cotton for durability or materials such as gauzy cotton or silk for opulence. For color, I use naturally dyed table linens. These linens are an easy way to add a bit of nature indoors, and even the boldest colors are warm and inviting. Naturally dyed hues work in harmony, so mixing and matching offer endless possibilities. In addition, when needed, folding tables can be camouflaged and transformed into grand tablescapes and buffets when properly utilizing linens.

Natural textiles create a warm, relaxed, and unique experience for your guests. I use oversized, undersized, overlapped, and textural linens. The linens presented here are 100 percent natural fibers, in an array of plant-dyed hues. While you can find my handcrafted table linens and napkins in my online shop, Silk & Willow, I encourage you to explore ways of crafting your own collection of table linens. Each table entry will list the linens included in that tablescape design. Consider each table linen as a fabric piece and determine how many fabric pieces you will need. Then, use my guide, Styling and Sizing Table Linens (page 20), to determine the length of the material required for your table size. You can create all the designs included using natural fabrics from your local fabric store or sustainable fabric sources online. Thrift stores and flea markets are also a good source for textiles and repurposing vintage linens. By simply cutting off the stitched edging

of an old tablecloth or naturally dyeing raw fabrics, you can repurpose a fabulous collection of new materials to utilize in your table designs.

Styling and Sizing Table Linens

Determining the size of the table linens you will need to style your table can feel overwhelming. With tables varying in length and width, and since tables are often combined for larger gatherings, it can be difficult to create an organic layered look with traditional standard-sized linens. In the illustration that follows, you will find the most used and requested table styles I create at Silk & Willow. Use the guide to re-create the table designs included, onto any size table.

STYLING AND SIZING
TABLE LINENS

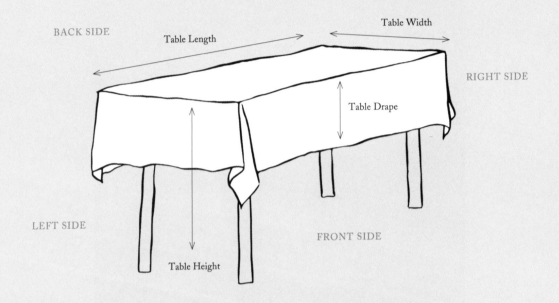

BACK SIDE

Table Length

Table Width

RIGHT SIDE

Table Drape

LEFT SIDE

FRONT SIDE

Table Height

STANDARD TABLE DRAPE

Table Length + {12 in [30.5 cm] x 2}

Table Width + {12 in [30.5 cm] x 2}

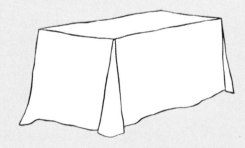

STANDARD DRAPE *with* PUDDLE ON ENDS

Table length + {table height x 2} +
1 to 1½ yd [91 to 137 cm]

Table width + {12 in [30.5 cm] x 2}

TABLE COVER: FLOOR-LENGTH DRAPE

Table length + {table height x 2}

Table width + {table height x 2}

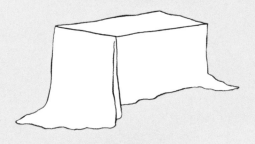

TABLE COVER: FLOOR LENGTH
with **PUDDLE ON ENDS**

Table length + {table height x 2} + 1½ yd [137 cm]

Table width + {table height x 2}

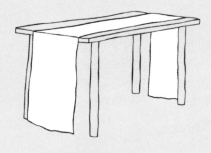

TABLE RUNNER

Floor Length: Table length +
{table height x 2}

TABLE RUNNER
with **GATHERING ON TOP**

Table length + 20 percent for gathering +
{table height x 2}

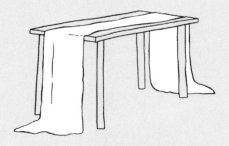

TABLE RUNNER *with* **GATHERING ON TOP** *and* **PUDDLE ON ENDS**

Table length + 20 percent for gathering +
{table height x 2} + 1½ yd [137 cm]

WATERFALL TABLE RUNNER

Same measurements as the *Table Runner with Gathering on Top and Puddle on Ends*

Placed diagonally from corner to corner

ROUND TABLE: TABLE RUNNER

Same measurements as
TABLE RUNNER for rectangle or square table.

Styling Napkins

When your guests are seated at the table, one of their first moves will likely be reaching for their napkin. While there is logic and symmetry to consider when placing your dinnerware, flatware, and glassware, your napkin placement is an opportunity to use your creativity! The placement of your napkin, along with its color and texture, will engage your guests as they await the meal to come.

There are no rules to dictate the placement of your napkin. Will your napkin be folded or unfolded, centered on the plate, or to the left of your plate? Maybe it's under the salad plate or draped across the chair back. Experiment with your napkin placements and notice how each placement changes the feel of the table. Use your napkin to wrap your flatware, place your napkin in between plates to contrast textures, gather your napkin to create a lofty backdrop for your menu, or drape your napkin to extend from the plate and over the edge of the table— each placement creates a unique experience for your guests to unfold.

The color of your napkin plays an integral role in your tablescape's overall design. Too many colors will make your table feel cluttered, so matching your napkin color to one other major element on the table, such as the florals or linens, will keep the table from becoming overworked. Your napkin colors can harmonize or emphasize one thing over another. It can be used to create depth and a sense of movement across the table.

Play with different cloth textures to add dimension to your dining experience. Gauzy cotton creates an ethereal, bohemian feel; pressed and folded feels more formal; silk is opulent; and soft, relaxed cotton is casual and inviting. Each texture can be used to balance and harmonize the other elements on the table.

Dinnerware

Dinnerware, as a broad term, refers to a set that typically includes dinner plates (10 to 11 in [25.4 to 28 cm] in diameter), salad plates (7½ to 8½ in [19 to 20.3 cm]), bowls (soup or cereal), and mugs. A more formal collection will substitute the mug for a cup and saucer. A simple, classic set of white dinnerware is the most versatile choice for any table. It will suit any occasion, and it acts as a neutral base for any color palette. I have a classic set of twelve white dinner plates, salad plates, bowls and mugs that I frequently use. When purchasing handmade ceramics, I purchase each piece of dinnerware separately,

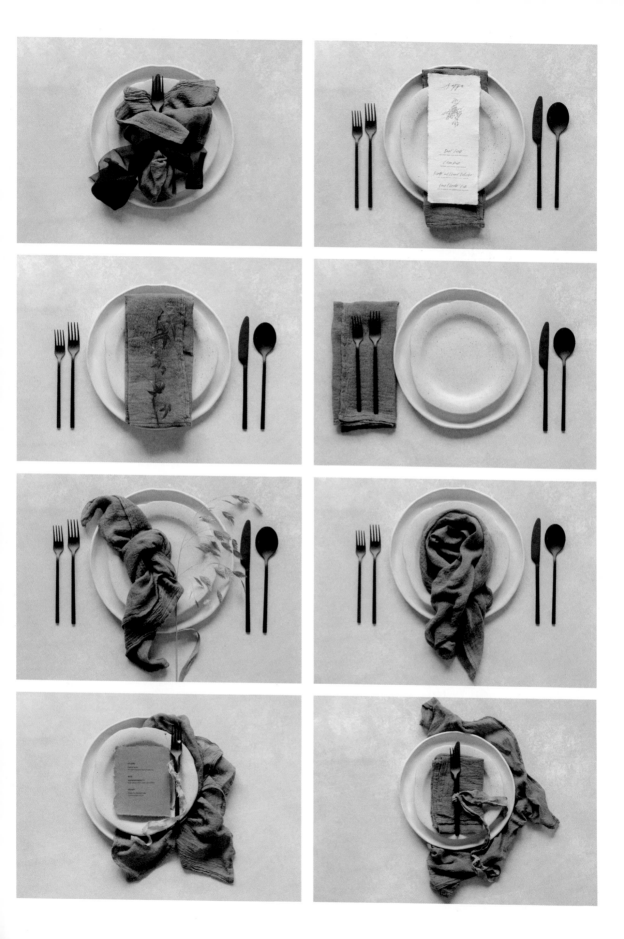

and I prefer to purchase my plates and bowls in sets of four or six. My full collection of white dinnerware varies in shades, shapes, and textures to offer variety. For larger gatherings, they can all be used together. I also have smaller sets of earth-toned and black plates in my collection. An earth-toned plate is warm and inviting; it plays well with other colors and offers variety. I adore black dinnerware for the allure and mystery they bring to the table. Black is a great way to play with contrast, and because darker colors recede, it works to highlight the other colors on the table. Stick with solid neutral hues for your dinner plates; this allows for versatility. Your salad plates and bowls are an opportunity to incorporate bolder colors, patterns, or textures to complement the style or theme of your table.

Glassware

Glassware refers to any type of glass drinking vessel. The types of glassware vary and are typically named to reflect the type of beverage to be served. "Stemware" is simply glassware with a bowl that rests on a stem, anchored by a base, and most often refers to wineglasses. For glassware, again, a clean and classic glass can be used for any occasion. Having a set of twelve water glasses and twelve wineglasses is a good starting point. Two sets of glassware, one with and one without a stem, is ideal. This creates visual interest and can easily differentiate your water glass from your wineglass. If storage space is limited, stemless wineglasses are a great option for versatility; they can be used for water, wine, or cocktails. As you expand your glassware collection, wineglasses specific to the type, such as white wine or red wine glasses, and celebratory glasses, such as champagne flutes and martini glasses, are great additions to have on hand. Simply changing your glassware to textured, colored, or beveled glasses can be all that's needed to change your table setting's mood and feel.

Flatware

Flatware comes in five-piece sets. They include a dinner fork, salad fork (which doubles as a dessert fork), soup spoon, dessert or slightly smaller teaspoon, and a knife. A set of steak knives and a butter knife that complements your flatware is a great way to round out your collection. Flatware is an investment, so it's best to pick an all-purpose set that can transition from everyday use to a more formal setting. My go-to is a matte silver flatware set. Matte silver works similarly to white—you can work it into any palette, and it can be used for any occasion. I use my vintage brass flatware to incorporate color, and for a clean, modern look, I use simple matte black flatware. Vintage flatware, found at antique stores and flea markets, is great for casual outdoor gatherings where you may be tempted to use plastic utensils. Choose flatware that resonates with your style and type of entertaining. From there, you can always build your collection and add in different patterns or finishes.

Accessories

I love to incorporate bowls, platters, boards, candles, salt dishes, vases, handmade paper, and ribbon into my table designs. When choosing your accessories, consider having a variety of textures to choose from. Smooth marble, shiny metal, textured clay, transparent glass, silky ribbon—each of these textures convey a feeling and add to the story of your tablescape. Choose platters, candleholders, and vases in varying heights—this is an easy way to add dimension to your table.

If you are going to invest in styling elements, a set of ceramic candleholders and a ceramic vase should be at the top of your list. With these versatile pieces, you can transform the mood of your table through the color of candle you choose or the size of the arrangement you place in your vase. You will notice that most of this book's styling elements are repeated on many of the tables. These are classic pieces in my collection that can be used for any occasion. Take a look around at the decorative elements you have in your house; your home decor may work great when incorporated into your table design. The crystal collection that decorates my home and studio becomes a shimmering accent for the Celestial Celebration (page 125), and for the Plant Oasis (page 149), a collection of houseplants are gathered and brought to one location. You will be surprised at what you can pull together when you take a new approach to designing your table.

Flowers

There's nothing more magical than a beautifully arranged floral centerpiece to add a sense of awe to your table design. This can be professionally created by a florist or wildly arranged with what you gather from your garden. I encourage you to take a walk and explore your outdoors for inspiration and foraging. A fallen branch or roadside weed simply placed in a vase can add charm to any tabletop.

Dry and save all and any flowers you get. Dried flowers can be mixed with fresh flowers or stand alone as a decorative element in many styling applications.

DRYING BOTANICALS

I am always collecting and gathering flowers, grasses, herbs, and branches for drying throughout each season. I focus on various colors, textures, and ease of drying when deciding which plants to collect and dry. My list includes favorites that I grow and gather from my property or seek from local florists and farmers. Also included are a few species not native to my area, but maybe to yours; each one is selected for its beauty and ease of drying. If you are new to growing flowers for drying, note that harvesting time varies for each plant, and many are best left to seed before harvesting.

FLOWERS *and* PODS

Amaranth	Delphinium	Poppy pods
Ammobium	Feverfew	Scabiosa
Astrantia	Field pennycress	Silver brunia
Baby's breath	Globe amaranth	Strawflower
Baptisia	Heather	Tansy
Bougainvillea	Hydrangea	Winged everlasting
Chamomile	Lunaria	Yarrow
Clematis	Nigella pods	Zinnia
Coreopsis	Pink pepperberries	

GRASS

Bunny tail
Flax
Foxtail
Peppergrass
Millet
Pampas grass
Plume reed grass
Tiger grass
Wild oats

HERBS

Lavender
Motherwort
Rosemary
Sage
Thyme

BRANCHES *and* LEAVES

Bittersweet
Boxwood
Eucalyptus
Fern
Magnolia
Smoke tree
Willow

No matter the occasion, gathering around your table is a time for nourishment and relishing treasured moments with family and friends. Setting your table with intention is a way to give gratitude for the opportunity to be together. Whether planning a casual daily meal or a special milestone celebration, following a few simple rules will give you confidence when designing and setting your table for any occasion.

The number one thing to remember when preparing your table setting is don't stress. Start with the basic necessities: dinnerware, flatware, and glassware. Then incorporate your natural styling elements and let your table transformation begin!

As with any styling project, design rules and techniques can be applied to make your table setting uniquely beautiful while serving its functional purpose. Don't let yourself be overwhelmed with what might feel like an endless list of table rules. Start with a few fundamentals and expand from there.

To start, place your dinner plate at the center of your setting, laid about 1 in [2.5 cm] in from the edge of the table. Ideally, your plates will be spaced with 15 in [38 cm] between each place setting to allow ample elbow room. A salad plate can be placed centered, on top of the dinner plate, or to the left of the fork (although I've never had enough room on the table for this option). If serving soup, place your bowl centered on top of the dinner plate, or if serving in addition to salad, place it centered on top of the salad plate.

There is only one steadfast rule I feel should be the foundation of every table setting, and that's the proper placement of flatware. The placement of your flatware should be both functional and familiar to your guests. It should align seamlessly with your meal, not add confusion or feel cumbersome. To achieve this flow, place utensils in the order they are used, from the outside in. Forks go to the left of the plate, and knives and spoons to the right. Place your dinner fork closest to the plate with your salad fork to the left of it. Place your knife closest to the plate, blade facing in, with your spoons directly to the right. There are a few variations to this placement. For casual gatherings, when all of your flatware is placed on your napkin, positioned to the left or on top of the dinner plate, use the following order: fork, knife (with the blade facing the fork), spoon. You can also gather the flatware together and tuck them into a napkin or tie them with ribbon or twine (see Styling Napkins, page 22). If you are serving salad after your main meal, you should switch your salad fork to the insde, closest to your plate. Do not clutter your table with unnecessary flatware. No salad or appetizer? No additional fork is needed. No soup? No spoon is needed. Don't worry, these rules will become second nature when practiced and used daily.

Traditionally, your flatware should align across the bottom with your dinner plate, be placed 1 in [2.5 cm] from the table edge, and the same distance from the sides of your plate. While I prefer alignment across the bottom, this is not a rigid rule. As long as your flatware is placed in the proper order, you can be flexible and creative with your alignment. Take a step back and do what works best with your unique table design.

When setting your glassware, always offer a water glass. Water should be served to each guest before they are seated at the table, be available throughout the meal, and be placed closest at hand, just above your dinner knife. When setting a formal table, it is customary to include a wineglass for each wine pairing with your meal. For most gatherings at home, I find that guests transition to the table with drinks in hand, so you may decide not to add additional glasses to your table setting. If you choose to include additional wineglasses at your table, they're best placed to the right of the water glass, outside in, in the order in which you intend to serve your wines.

Remember these suggestions outlined here are to be used as a guide. If your decorative elements, such as flowers or candles, interfere with the exact placement, a little tweaking is always acceptable. Be flexible with the placement of your glassware by adapting it to your available space and the beverages to be served.

Setting a natural table is about creating a warm and inviting space—perfectly imperfect, just like nature. With the subtle hues from nature and outdoor elements you gather, the magic of your table setting will bring warmth and comfort to all who experience your presentation.

HOW TO USE THIS BOOK

In the following pages you'll discover fifteen tables, along with how-tos for recipes, floral arrangements, natural dyeing, and other projects that will elevate any tablescape. Each table included is designed with my unique approach, formed from a love and appreciation for an eclectic mix of styles, combined with a practical approach of utilizing classic styling elements.

Every table design began with inspiration from the outdoors; nature was my guide. From there, I reflect on the mood and energy I want to convey for each table. It may be simple and reflective, as in my wabi-sabi-influenced Afternoon Tea (page 137), or opulent and moody like the Modern Dutch Master (page 53). Each table is unique, but they were all created with the same approach of using natural materials to add beauty and intrigue to the presentation.

The tables you'll find in this book should be a launching point for your own table design journey. If you don't have all the styling elements needed to replicate the table designs included here, I encourage you to get creative with what you do have. Use the color palette, shape, scale, and placement of the styling elements as your guide. Then, look around inside and outside to see what you have to fit each space on the table. Additionally, I encourage you to combine what you've learned from each table, pull together the different projects and tips throughout this book, and have fun creating your own signature tablescape.

Gathering with friends and family is a time to celebrate, no matter the occasion. Even a simple impromptu get-together can be enhanced by dressing the table with linens, adding a few styling elements, and incorporating elements of the natural world. My hope is that this book will encourage and inspire you to examine nature and delight in the possibilities it brings to the table.

TABLE
DESIGNS

WEEKEND BRUNCH

Welcome the day with the scents of warm pastries, freshly brewed coffee, and citrus lofting in the air. While gazing out at the garden, a quaint summer brunch is the perfect recipe for a leisurely weekend get-together.

STYLING ELEMENTS

Gray cotton table runner

Indigo cotton napkins

Handmade ceramic black plates

Handmade ceramic white bowls

Silver flatware

Gray coffee mug

Classic juice glass

Vintage glass milk bottle

Ceramic pitchers

Assorted ceramic dishes

Garden flowers, wildflowers, herbs

When you're choosing the color palette for your brunch table linens, consider the menu items you are serving. Your food becomes a styling element when placed throughout your table, and complementing their hues with the linens you choose creates a well-balanced table. I love using charcoal-gray linens in my tablescapes—it's a dark, neutral layer that works to highlight the food elements featured on the table. Dark-colored dinnerware works in the same manner to accentuate the colors and shapes in the meal to be served.

Table runners are a great way to add color, texture, and movement to your table design without fully covering your tabletop. Draping your runner from corner to corner, rather than the more traditional method of running it down the middle of the table, creates movement and adds a twist to your presentation. In the table shown here, a waterfall effect is achieved by gathering your material on the tabletop and then letting the material flow over the edge and puddle onto the floor. This allows you to experience both the table's natural texture and the softness of the gauzy linen.

Using fruit as a design element is an easy way to add color and texture to your table, while also offering your guests plenty of snacking options. Placed throughout the table, the plums, blueberries, blackberries, grapes, cherries, apricots, and oranges add a variety of gorgeous colors, and the repetition creates a natural pattern and sense of movement across the table.

Indigo napkins are neatly folded upon each plate, and a bowl of homemade granola and fruit on top eagerly awaits each guest. The blue is soothing while simultaneously stimulating when paired with its complementary color, orange. Complementary colors, ones that sit opposite on a color wheel, work

right To add dimension to your tablescape, choose cake pedestals as an alternative to flat serving platters. They add height to your table and can be stacked if table space is limited.

harmoniously to intensify each other, thus making blue the perfect color to energize the orange citrus hues placed throughout the table. These two colors are just enough to make the table feel vibrant without being overpowering.

The casual setting of brunch is an opportunity to experiment with mixing your dinnerware. My cherished ceramics collection is composed of a wide range of products from different artists, and they vary in shape, size, color, and texture. I love to use a mixed assortment of pieces to bring character to the table. Have fun mixing your dinnerware; this is an opportunity to display a medley of your favorite pieces and let your personal style shine!

left Create a waterfall effect with your table runner by draping the runner off each corner of your table. This not only creates a beautiful visual, but it allows for additional seating on the ends of the table.

above Tall cylinder jars are great for storing extra granola or cereal. The filled jars become a table display without taking up much space.

FOXFIRE RUSTIC PLUM GALETTE

Foxfire Mountain House is an eclectic inn and restaurant nestled in the Catskills. Whether you're snuggled by the stone fireplace in winter or sitting by the lily pond in summer, Foxfire Mountain House is an enchanting place to unplug and enjoy the surroundings. The beautifully restored glass pavilion, overlooking the property's pond and woodland trails, was the perfect location to host our late morning brunch. The relaxed and modern bohemian vibe, along with the seasonal food preparations, are inspired and guided by nature. Tim Trojian, their chef and co-owner, shares a bit of the Foxfire experience with his flavorful and flaky plum galette recipe. This seasonal treat for the senses will surely lure your guests to the table.

Serves 8 to 10

GALETTE PASTRY DOUGH

3 cups [420 g] all-purpose flour

¼ tsp table salt

1½ sticks frozen unsalted butter

¼ cup [60 ml] ice water

FILLING

1 cup [200 g] sugar

½ cup [60 g] ground almonds

3 Tbsp all-purpose flour

2 eggs, individually beaten

5 Tbsp [70 g] unsalted butter, at cool room temperature

2½ lb [1.2 kg] black plums, halved, pitted, and cut into ½ in [12 mm] wedges

½ cup [150 g] apricot preserves for glazing the plums

¼ cup [25 g] sliced almonds

Step 1   To make the galette pastry dough, add the flour and salt to the bowl of a food processor and grate the frozen butter into it. Pulse to process for 5 to 8 seconds; the butter should still be in visible pieces. Add the ice water and pulse again for about 5 more seconds, just until the dough comes together; the butter should still be visible. To make the dough by hand, whisk together the flour and salt in a bowl, add the grated butter, and use two forks to blend the mixture together until it has a pebble-like quality. Add the ice water and mix until the dough comes together.

Step 2   Remove the dough from the bowl and gather it into a ball. On a lightly floured surface, roll out the dough into a 16 in [40.5 cm] square, medium thick. Transfer the square to a large, heavy, well-floured baking sheet. Chill the dough until firm, about 20 minutes.

Step 3   Position a rack in the middle of the oven. Preheat the oven to 400°F [200°C].

cont'd

Step 4　To make the filling, combine ½ cup [100 g] of the sugar with the ground almonds, flour, 1 beaten egg, and 2 Tbsp of the butter in a mixing bowl. Mix well and spread this mixture evenly over the dough to within 2 in [5 cm] of the edge. Arrange the plum wedges on top and dot with the remaining 3 Tbsp of butter. Sprinkle all but 1 tsp of the remaining sugar over the fruit. Fold the edge of the dough up over the plums to create a 2 in [5 cm] border. (If the dough feels cold and firm, wait for a few minutes until it softens to prevent it from cracking.) Brush the edges with the remaining beaten egg, sprinkle with the remaining 1 tsp of sugar, and top with the sliced almonds.

Step 5　Bake for about 1 hour, until the plums are soft and the crust is golden brown. The juice from the plums will combine with the sugar and thicken; that is the best indication that the galette is fully cooked. If any juices have leaked onto the baking sheet, slide a knife under the galette to release it from the sheet. Evenly brush the apricot preserves over the hot fruit; brush some up onto the crust too, if desired. Let the galette cool to room temperature before serving.

right Flowers and herbs, cut straight from the garden and wildly placed in a vase, bring a fresh summer feel to your table.

MODERN DUTCH MASTER

This tablescape draws inspiration from Dutch master painters of the seventeenth century. Attention to detail, the interplay of light on flowers and fabrics, and highlighting the beauty in nature are hallmarks of Dutch master still lifes. Here, the floral centerpiece is the focal point.

STYLING ELEMENTS

Blue-gray cotton table cover

Mauve cotton napkins

Matte black plates

Vintage brass flatware

Smoke-colored wineglasses

Beveled water glass

Matte black ceramic candleholders

Black iron candleholders

Gray and blue beeswax taper candles

Menus, 4 by 9 in [10 by 23 cm]

Ribbon detail, 1 yd [91 cm] per setting

Assorted fruits and vegetables

Flower arrangement (see page 61)

Clusters of tall candles flank the floral arrangement, intensifying its visual impact. Upon viewing your abundantly beautiful centerpiece, your guests will feel transported in time as they marvel at your masterpiece.

The table starts with a dusty blue-gray table cover. The muted blue reads as a neutral backdrop, allowing the mauve-colored napkins to pop. You can be flexible here; any shade of gray will work as your base table linen. In selecting your napkin color, draw inspiration from your flowers and fruits. In this case, the wine-colored grapes, pink snapdragons, and purple poppies guided my napkin color. Repeating the same hues in different areas on the table is a gentle way to keep the eye moving through the tablescape. To prevent your table from becoming too busy, choose monochromatic plates and glassware. Matte black plates and smoky gray stemware fade into the background, leaving the flowers' colors to shine.

Evoking the experience of viewing a Dutch still life, this table is about discovery. Guests will be enchanted and drawn to the many compotes and bowls overflowing with fruits and berries. Plums, figs, grapes, pears, and pomegranates add to the sultry palette and create an opportunity for your guests to nibble as they await the first course.

above Leave some fruits whole to add sculptural shapes. Dried fruits are an excellent option if you want to include produce that isn't in season. Instead of using a knife, consider tearing pomegranates and loaves of bread into small pieces to create an organic look.

above Create a seamless and cohesive feel by carrying elements of your tablescape theme onto other tables in your space. Entry tables, end tables, coffee tables, and buffet tables are all design opportunities. Use wood cutting boards as cheese platters and cake pedestals to showcase fruit; this creates layers of height, adds visual intrigue, and offers your guests something to enjoy in every corner. Jewel-toned napkins or small styling fabrics draped across a cake pedestal add color, texture, and movement while keeping your fruits nestled in place.

CREATING YOUR DUTCH MASTER
with FRUITS AND VEGETABLES

Kiana Underwood, the founder and floral designer behind Tulipina, is a master of color, structure, and movement. Kiana is internationally renowned for her bespoke floral designs and has been named one of the top wedding florists in the world by Harper's Bazaar. *In her arrangements and table designs, she often uses fruit and vegetables to add a level of interest and sophistication. Fruits and vegetables can add pops of color, unique shapes, and textures not typically found in a floral centerpiece.*

Kiana emphasizes that proper tools are the foundation for creating a successful centerpiece. Sharp pruning shears won't damage the stems and will allow your flowers to soak up the water they need. She recommends avoiding floral foam, as working with it creates dust that is harmful to us, and it is a pollutant to the environment. Her signature tool is the floral pin frog (kenzan); they come in many styles and shapes and can be held tightly in place with floral putty. To create an arrangement that evokes the Dutch masters, she suggests playing with complementary colors, ingredients of varying shapes and sizes, mixing in wildflowers with exotic botanicals, and embracing the drooping flower that wilts and bends onto the table. "Your end result will look like you went into a wonderful garden and picked one of each variety," Kiana says.

MATERIALS

Floral pin frog

Floral putty

Compote vase

Fruit or vegetables on stems and branches (such as grapes, tomatoes, currants, wild berries, kumquats, or olives)

Flowers (such as peonies, poppies, ranunculus, delphinium, allium, and snapdragons)

Floral clippers

Vines or greenery (optional)

cont'd

Step 1 Secure the floral pin frog with floral putty inside the vessel.

Step 2 Begin with heavier elements such as your fruit bunches, branches, or vegetables on a vine, as they are the heaviest elements of this arrangement and should be well secured in the floral pin frog. Place them in the vessel and let them drape and spill over the rim. Once the foundation is secure, you can start adding the flowers.

Step 3 Choose a large flower, such as a peony, to showcase as the focal point. This can be placed left of center, close to the edge of your vessel.

Step 4 Next, create height by adding one of the longer floral stems, such as a poppy or snapdragon, placed toward the upper right. From there, nestle everything else in layers and clusters, around the focal flowers.

Step 5 Examine the arrangement from a distance, as your perspective on what it looks like when you move away from it can be quite different. If you need to fill in gaps or add movent to your arrangement, vines or greenery are a great addition.

right No matter the size of your gathering, adding a menu to each place setting will add a finishing touch to your well-appointed table. Your paper's texture, color, and typography are opportunities to add to your overall design. For our Dutch feast, a clean and simple layout is an elegant choice. Handmade paper with a soft deckled edge adds a bit of romance and plays beautifully against the contemporary black plates.

To highlight the mauve-colored napkins, the color is repeated using silk ribbon as a decorative accent on the menus. The ribbon, pulled through the menu, adds a unique layer of texture. Simply use a utility knife to create a slit in the menu paper and pull the ribbon through the paper halfway, letting the ribbon drape down from both sides of the paper. The silk captures the light, creates a statement, and adds a sensory experience for your guests to enjoy.

When using deckled-edge handmade paper in your home printer, it helps to iron the deckled edges flat, on medium heat, before feeding into your inkjet printer. Smoothing the edges flat with an iron helps prevent the ink from hitting the paper's uneven edges and smearing ink on your menu.

FEAST

SALAD
baby arugula with cherry tomatoes, pine nuts,
shaved parmesan, and lemon olive oil vinaigrette

MAIN
Parmesan and herb encrusted salmon with lemon
basil butter, potato puree and roasted vegetables

DESSERT
Flourless chocolate cake with pomegranate sauce

BOTANICAL BIRTHDAY

A birthday or milestone is made extra special by adding natural handcrafted details to the celebration table.

STYLING ELEMENTS

Botanical-dyed sheer silk table runner

Gray cotton gauzy napkins

White ceramic dessert plates

Silver flatware

Vintage water glasses

Wood trivet

Natural beeswax candles

Birthday cake

Potted herbs

Flowers, dried arrangement

This birthday table has minimal styling elements, but each is crafted with love and intention for the guest of honor. The natural details of the table runner, dried floral centerpiece, and cake are neither fussy nor overcomplicated; this refined simplicity adds a decorative touch and allows the story of the day to unfold without distractions.

Sheer silk fabric can be transformed with natural dye from flowers. To create my botanical print table runner, flowers are placed directly onto silk fabric, tightly rolled, and then steamed for hours. The colors from the flowers are infused into the silk, and the petal shapes become a beautiful floral pattern to add to the botanical-inspired celebration. Draping a silk fabric runner off the end of the table in a waterfall fashion creates a focal point that draws attention to the table.

A centerpiece of dried flowers arranged in a vintage flower frog is a unique and easy way to add beauty and color to your table. Collecting and drying flowers throughout the year is a great way to have natural elements on hand, in any season, to draw inspiration and bring nature to your tablescape. Vintage flower frogs, which can be found at thrift stores or antique shops, hold flowers easily and make a beautiful presentation. In a pinch, chicken wire rolled into a planter works well too. There is no

right or wrong way to arrange; just add flowers until your flower frog is full. Try not to overthink your arrangement; the more organic the shape, the better.

When choosing your plates, I suggest selecting colors that complement your dried floral centerpiece. Alternatively, white plates offer a neutral backdrop, keeping the attention on the delightful cake to be served. In selecting your glasses and flatware, anything goes. This table is all about utilizing what you have and making the table beautiful with just a few unique details.

above Add to your room decor by wrapping potted herbs with cut fabric or cotton napkins.

CAKE DECORATING
with FLOWERS AND HERBS

The birthday cake is always the highlight of our family birthday gatherings. Weeks before their birthdays, my daughters and I begin to ponder the flavors and decor for their birthday cakes. When they were younger, I would theme their cakes to coincide with their interests at the time: a merry-go-round cake, teapot-shaped cake, a fairy wonderland cake, horse cake, and bowling pin cake are a few of the standouts. As they got older, they would select their flavor and await the surprise of what I would create. This tradition has created many cherished memories.

For this project you'll be decorating a homemade or bakery-bought cake with flowers and herbs. If you don't have a garden to cut from, you can buy flowers from a local farm or florist that grows organic blooms. Pots of fresh herbs can be found in most grocery stores and nurseries. Choose herbs with long, soft stems; this will allow you to bend the stems around the cake. For this project, I use thyme, but feel free to get creative and try oregano, marjoram, or tarragon. I recommend using white icing, but any neutral, light-colored icing will work.

MATERIALS

Homemade or store-bought cake with white frosting

Fresh thyme or other herb of your choice

Edible fresh or dried flowers

Step 1 Start by placing an herb sprig around the base of one side of the cake. Do the same around the top of the cake on the opposite side. Press the herbs slightly into the frosting to hold them in place.

Step 2 Cut additional pieces of the herb. Loosely connect the herbs from the top piece to the bottom piece, creating a spiral around the cake.

Step 3 Once the herbs are placed, start adding the flowers; use fresh and/or dried flower heads. You should use only organically grown edible flowers, such as bachelor's button, calendula, chamomile, nasturtium, pansies, roses, and violets, to name a few. Cut the flower heads, leaving ¼ in [6 mm] of stem. The stem can be pressed into the cake to hold the flower head in place. Just a few flowers on each side are all that's needed to add pops of color to the cake.

above Wrap your birthday gift with a ribbon matching the color of the flowers on your cake. The coordinating colors will make the gift a part of your party decor.

right Use natural beeswax candles to decorate your cake. The sweet smell of natural beeswax will loft through the air and no one will be harmed by any candle drippings on the cake.

DATE NIGHT IN

Celebrate romance with soft pink hues, the warm glow of candlelight, and overlapping layers of texture in this romantic table for two. Perfect for an anniversary, Valentine's Day, or a date night in, this table is a lovely centerpiece for a special occasion.

STYLING ELEMENTS

White cotton table cover

Blush cotton table runner

Pink avocado-dyed cotton napkins (see page 83)

White dinner plates

White salad plates

Silver flatware

Stemless wineglasses

White ceramic salt dish with pink Himalayan salt

Pink glass votive holders

White ceramic flower frog

White ceramic bowls with metal flower frogs

Ribbon detail, 30 in [76 cm] length per setting

Flowers, wild Queen Anne's lace

Start with a natural white table cover as a base, and then add a hint of color with a soft blush-colored table runner. Choosing a quiet, subtle monochromatic color palette for the table will direct your attention to one another. Use your imagination as you gather and fold the linens on the table—little tucks, billowing folds, and a table leg peeking out will help conjure a sense of allure.

The plates in this tablescape are white and organically shaped, adding to the softness on the table. For your napkins, try a gauzy texture with frayed edges for an unexpected twist. Tuck your flatware into your napkin and tie with a silky-smooth ribbon to create the sensory pleasure of "unwrapping" before the first course.

While I love using roses to foster a sense of romance, it's also nice to take advantage of what's free and abundant around you. For this presentation, I used Queen Anne's lace, which is a beautiful "weed" found alongside roads and parking lots and fields throughout the summer. Small arrangements placed around the room add a delicate, lacy touch to your romantic get-together. Place single stems in little glass bottles or gather the stems in a bowl using a flower frog to elevate a simple bloom into a showcase piece.

AVOCADO-DYED NAPKINS

My natural dyeing journey began in my kitchen, using food items cooked in my stainless steel pots to create a color. I love experimenting with different natural materials to create unique colors, and this simple technique using avocado pits creates a lovely blush hue.

Your home cooking pot will work for this project since the dye is made from a food by-product, but you may prefer to have a dedicated dye pot for natural dyeing, as some colors may stain your cookware. Try your local thrift store or garage sales to find inexpensive pots for dyeing.

The avocado pits for this recipe can be used at any stage from fresh to dry, but always make sure to thoroughly clean them with water and a sponge to remove the avocado pulp before using. Collect discarded pits from friends and family, or ask a local restaurant if they can save them for you. Once they are cleaned, you can keep them on your counter or windowsill until they are completely dry and then store them in a jar, or you can put clean, fresh or dried pits in a sealed container directly in the freezer to store for future use.

The more avocado pits you use, the darker and more saturated the color will be. Leaving the dyebath overnight will also deepen the hue. I recommend using ten avocado pits for 2 sq yd [1.7 sq m] of fabric.

I use prewashed cheesecloth as my fabric in this recipe, but you can use any 100 percent natural fabric, such as silk, cotton, or linen. This is also a great project for repurposing any lightly stained linens. The natural dye can mask the stain and you'll have a new set of linens!

MATERIALS

2 sq yd [1.7 sq m] prewashed grade 40 cheesecloth

10 avocado pits, fresh, dried, or directly from the freezer

Large stainless steel or aluminum pot (lid recommended but not required)

Heat-resistant rubber gloves or slotted spoon

Step 1 Prepare the cheesecloth by opening any folds and soaking it in room-temperature tap water for 1 hour to saturate the fabric and open the fibers to accept the dye. Set aside while preparing the dyebath.

cont'd

Step 2 Add the avocado pits to the pot and fill the pot three-quarters full with water. The pot should be large enough to allow the material to move freely in the water.

Step 3 Place the pot on the stove, turn the heat to medium-high, cover with a lid, and bring the water to a boil.

Step 4 Once the water comes to a rolling boil, turn the heat down to low and continue to simmer for 30 minutes. Next, turn off the heat and let sit to cool.

Step 5 When the dyebath is cool, remove the avocado pits using a slotted spoon or your rubber-glove-covered hands (avocado pits are high in tannins, which can irritate your skin). The leftover avocado pits can be composted.

Step 6 Add the prepared cheesecloth (from step 1) to the dyebath. Turn the heat to medium and bring to a light simmer for 40 minutes. Stir occasionally. Observe as the color is infused into the fabric. Once you achieve your desired shade, turn off the heat and let cool. Leave the material in the dyebath overnight to intensify the color.

Step 7 Once the dyebath cools to room temperature, remove the fabric from the dyebath and rinse thoroughly with cool tap water. Hand-wash with pH-neutral soap and lay flat or hang to dry. Note, once your material is washed and dried, it will be slightly lighter in color than what it appears when it is wet.

CARE

Hand-wash or wash in the washing machine on a gentle cycle with cold water and pH-neutral soap. To dry, lay flat, hang, or tumble dry on low. Some shrinkage may occur in the dryer.

CREATING ADDITIONAL COLORS

Natural hues can be extracted from many of the foods and spices in your pantry or food waste. Using food waste to create color is a gratifying way to make something beautiful from what would otherwise be thrown away. Starting with step 2, experiment with swapping the avocado pits with avocado skins for pale peach hues, onion skins for yellows and corals, used tea bags for tans, coffee grounds for browns, turmeric and pomegranate rinds for yellows, or annatto seeds for orange-yellow. Each of these food items are substantive dyes, which means they contain tannins that work as a mordant and allow the color to bond naturally to your fabric. Don't worry so much about amounts and measurements; simply use what you have and experiment with the results. As a general rule, let a 1:1 ratio of dye material to the fabric's dry weight be a starting point to guide you.

OCEAN INSPIRED

If you long for the rhythmic sound of crashing waves, picturesque views, and sand beneath your feet, you can capture that ambiance with an ocean-inspired tablescape (no matter where you live).

STYLING ELEMENTS

White cotton table cover

Light-gray sheer silk runner

Blue-gray silk napkins

White dinner plates

Blue marble-glazed salad plates

Silver flatware

Classic water glasses

Classic wineglasses

White pillar candles

Sea coral

Menu (see page 95)

The soft watercolor palette of creamy whites, dusty blues, and grays, together with ocean textures, such as shells and coral, will conjure the serenity of a seaside setting. This table is a lovely way to highlight a menu featuring the bounty of the sea, whether you're serving raw oysters, steamed mussels, a feast of lobster, or the catch of the day.

To bring your ocean-inspired tablescape to life, focus on three main elements: color, decor, and food. The subtle palette used here conjures the airiness of walking in the sand and watching rolls of waves rush in. Responsibly sourced ocean coral, found in all shapes and sizes, is the perfect natural decor element to feel transported to the seaside. Alternatively, clusters of large seashells, such as pearl nautiluses, Australian trumpets, pearlized jade turbos, or mother-of-pearl shells will make a beautiful coastal display.

The base of your table begins with a natural white cotton table cover with plenty of extra fabric to generously puddle on the floor. The material is pressed for a finished look, highlighting the movement of the silky-smooth table runner. When laying your silk runner down the center of your table, bunch and overlap the silk to create a ruffle of layers. The vision of rippling waves is the desired effect. In

varying heights, pillar candles offer a warm, intimate glow and a nice contrast to the textured coral, shells, or other natural seaside materials. Repeating the pattern of candle clusters and coral across the entire table creates a dramatic presentation. If your supplies are limited, you can achieve the same coastal feel with a smaller arrangement created at quarter scale and placed in the middle of the table as a centerpiece.

left Here, a greenhouse is transformed with draping white fabric to create the backdrop for our ocean-inspired table design. Fabric panels purchased by the yard can be draped in any location to camouflage environments that distract from your table theme.

The dinner plates are a pearlescent white, and the salad plates, for the first course, are hand-glazed in watercolor blues. Slightly tucked and draped between the two plates are blue-gray silk napkins. The silky napkins add an opulent texture to the tablescape. The glassware and matte silver flatware have a clean, classic design that fades into the background, drawing your attention to the custom menus featuring a feast of ocean fare.

above When you're presenting large clusters of candles in your table decor, choose unscented candles. While a lightly scented candle can sometimes add to the ambiance, an abundance of scented candles on the dining table can be overwhelming and compete with the flavors of your meal.

Through texture, movement, color, and natural oceanic accents, you set the mood and essence of the sea in every detail. If weather permits, open your windows and doors to let the outdoor breeze move across your table, transporting your guests to a seaside soirée.

above Light and airy silk napkins, draped off the table and blowing in the breeze, evoke the feel of ocean waves. While sheer silk fabric is not a typical fabric choice for napkins, it will serve its purpose, intrigue your guests, and create a decorative element to remember.

Menu

Menu

Petite Crab Cakes
kale, fennel, horseradish mustard aioli

Chilean Sea Bass
whipped potatoes, champagne truffle sauce

Flourless Chocolate Cake
hand spun vanilla bean ice cream, chocolate

DESIGNING A CUSTOM MENU

When you're planning an intimate gathering with friends and family, consider adding the personal touch of designing a menu for each place setting. For me, the menu is less about informing the guests about the meal to be served and more about creating a special experience that unfolds the moment you are seated at the table.

A beautifully designed menu will give your table a more polished, thoughtfully executed look. Here, I use the contrasting textures of standard cardstock, which can be purchased at any art or business supply store, and handmade paper, which comes in a variety of sizes and can be purchased at art supply stores or artisans' shops online. Then, each menu is wrapped with naturally dyed sheer organza silk fabric to complement my table palette. For this project, any lightweight sheer fabric in your color palette will do (see Resources, page 216, for fabric store options).

The menu template included will create a 3½ by 5 in [9 by 12 cm] menu with a 7½ by 5½ in [19 by 14 cm] folder for your menu. Use the template on page 218 or experiment with creating your own custom-sized menu. In addition to adding color and texture to your table's design, your custom menus offer your guests a special memento of the magical dinner you created.

MATERIALS

8½ by 11 in [21.6 by 27.9 cm] cardstock
(1 sheet per 4 menus)

Printer and/or calligraphy pen

Handmade paper
(determined by the number of menus)

Sheer fabric
(determined by the number of menus)

Twine

Step 1 Plan your dinner menu and determine the number of guests you intend to serve. It's always best to make two or three extra menus in case mistakes happen during the production, or extra guests arrive. For my 3½ by 5 in [9 by 12 cm] menus, I can make four menus on one 8½ by 11 in [21.6 by 27.9 cm] sheet of cardstock. I have six place settings, so I will make eight menus on two sheets of cardstock; this will give me two extra menus.

Step 2 Starting with an 8½ by 11 in [21.6 by 27.9 cm] document on a computer, create a text box to your menu size specifications. Type your menu text, then copy and paste that text box to create four menus within the document. Once complete, using a printer, print onto the cardstock and cut out each individual menu. Alternatively, you can cut the blank cardstock to size and use hand calligraphy to write each menu.

Step 3 Use the handmade paper to create a folder for the menu. First, measure the folder size by doubling the width of the menu and add ½ in [12 mm] to the menu's width and height. For my 3½ by 5 in [9 by 12 cm] menu, my handmade paper folder will be 7½ by 5 ½ in [19 by 14 cm].

Step 4 Tear or cut the handmade paper to size. Tearing the paper creates a soft deckled edge. Next, fold the handmade paper in half, lengthwise, to create the folder. The cardstock menu will tuck inside the handmade paper folder.

cont'd

Step 5 Choose a lightweight sheer fabric that will coordinate with your design palette. Here, I use a dusty-blue organza silk; it's light and airy and not too bulky when wrapped around the menu. Each fabric piece should be measured by calculating your menu's height by four times the menu's width. In this case my cardstock menu is 3½ by 5 in [9 by 12 cm], so my fabric pieces are 14 by 5 in [35.5 by 12 cm].

When cutting your fabric to size, don't worry about being exact, a little unevenness adds a more interesting, natural look.

Step 6 With the menu inside the handmade paper folder, start in the front and wrap the sheer fabric twice around the folder.

Step 7 Finish off with twine. You can double- or triple-wrap your twine around the menu and folder and tie a loose bow or knot.

NOTE
For my menus, I used a combination of hand lettering and a clean sans serif type for the menu text. The hand calligraphy creates a beautiful contrast to highlight the menu courses or main ingredients. If you don't feel comfortable with your own handwriting abilities, you can use fonts created by calligraphy artists to create a custom look. Two of my go-tos for digital hand calligraphy are House of Modern Letters and Rare Bird Specimen I and II, created by Written Word Calligraphy.

GARDEN GATHERING

Outdoor dining is a relaxed, informal way to enjoy time with friends and family. For this table, pair delicious, simple foods with seasonal flowers for a garden-fresh, easygoing look.

STYLING ELEMENTS

Pale-yellow cotton table runner

Pale-yellow cotton napkins

Handmade ceramic white plates

Varied vintage silver flatware

Hand-blown glass goblets

Glass water pitcher

White ceramic salt dishes

Ceramic votive candleholders

Handmade botanical bundle with palo santo (see page 107)

Handmade ceramic vases

Flowers, garden

The beauty of this table is that it requires little effort. You don't need to add elaborate details or spend countless hours preparing in order to create a gorgeous garden table. For my table, I used vibrant yellow flowers and fresh greens from the garden as colorful styling elements. In the height of summer, gardens, farm stands, and farmers' markets are abundant with flowers that will instantly elevate your presentation.

Simple flower arrangements create a festive impact when loosely gathered and repeated across your table. Using multiple vases in varying heights gives the illusion of movement, and sunny yellow blooms always evoke a cheerful atmosphere. Dyer's chamomile is abundant in my garden and a go-to for brightening my summer tables. You can create a similar look with other yellow flowers from the Asteraceae family: Chamomile, cosmos, daisy, coreopsis, and tansy are just a few examples—alternatively, small potted plants from your local nursery will work as well. The key to creating a bold impact with a single flower variety is by repeating it across your table.

Lightly hued linens allow the colors of the flowers and the outdoor landscape to shine. Simply place your runner across the center of the table and lay

your napkins loosely on each plate to hang over the table's edge. The warm hues and soft draping of the fabric will welcome guests to the table. The botanical-inspired palo santo stick bundles (see page 107) on top of each place setting adds a touch of magic to your tablescape, and also serves as a surprise gift for your guests to take home with them after the meal.

For this family-style dinner, platters and bowls with seasonal greens and easy grilled recipes are passed and shared. For dining, with multiple courses served at once, a dinner plate is all that's needed for this casual and communal setting. Vintage flatware, easily found at flea markets, thrift stores, and antique stores, is a lovely way to add a unique

above You can sprinkle seasonal delights and pops of color into your presentation by adding fresh fruits, herbs, or vegetables, such as thinly sliced cucumbers, to your water pitcher.

right As in nature, repetition creates a natural pattern and the illusion of movement. Repeat items on your table, such as flower arrangements or clusters of candles, for a dynamic impact that keeps your eye engaged.

personalized touch to your table. Have fun mixing patterns, but ideally, your color tone and sizing should be consistent. Continue to add to your collection, and you'll never be short of a fork when extra guests arrive.

I like to use votive candleholders to protect flames from the breeze and create a warm, intimate glow as the sun fades. I also suggest keeping a basket with blankets beside the table to add an even cozier vibe—it invites your guests to stay into the evening, snuggling up as the sun goes down.

top left The pale-yellow table runner and napkins, dyed with onion skins, were created by repurposing white cotton linens stained from a mishap at a previous get-together (see Creating Additional Colors on page 85 for dyeing with onion skins).

BOTANICAL BUNDLES
with PALO SANTO

Handmade bundles with dried botanicals, palo santo sticks, and a quartz crystal make a beautiful display on your table and a thoughtful gift for your guests.

I gather and dry flowers, herbs, and branches from my surroundings throughout the year, so I always have a variety of dried botanicals on hand for crafting and creating. My crystal collection is vast from years of collecting, but it started small, with just a few quartz crystals. Now, I always keep a bowl of quartz crystals in my studio. Quartz is the most powerful healing stone, and its ability to amplify energy adds high vibrations to your room. Palo santo, known for its cleansing energy, is lovely to have on hand for adding a sweet healing aroma to the air.

MATERIALS

Flowers and herbs, dried

Palo santo sticks, ethically harvested

Hemp or nettle twine

Quartz crystals

Step 1 Using dried flowers, herbs, or grass (see chart on page 27 for suggestions), create a botanical bed for the palo santo sticks to rest upon.

Step 2 Place 2 palo santo sticks onto the dried flowers and arrange them into a mini bundle.

Step 3 Wrap twine multiple times around the dried botanicals and palo santo to hold them together.

Step 4 Add a quartz crystal on top and wrap twice more, finishing it off with a loose bow.

NOTES

Have a few loose palo santo sticks on hand in a small bowl or dish for evening burning. Use a candle or lighter to light one end of a palo santo stick. Hold at about a 45-degree angle, pointing the tip down toward the flame, allowing it to burn for about 30 seconds to 1 minute, and then blow it out. Set your palo santo stick on a fire-resistant dish or in a bowl with sand to safely hold your stick secure. In addition to adding an earthy, sweet aroma to the air, the fresh palo santo smoke works well to keep mosquitoes and other flying insects at bay.

When finished with your palo santo, place the stick in a fireproof bowl to naturally burn out or run the burning tip underwater to extinguish. Let dry completely before lighting again. Never leave burning sticks unattended.

Turn to your surroundings for inspiration! Flowers, grasses, branches, and leaves can all be incorporated into your garden table designs. If you don't have access to a backyard, take a walk, or visit your local garden nursery or farmers' market. Inspiration can be found in the cracks of a sidewalk, wispy branches, or a fallen seed pod.

FUN AND FANCIFUL

This festive table is perfect for any special gathering that involves children. Whether you are setting your table for a birthday party, baby shower, or just a special playdate with little ones, the cheerful attraction of pom-poms and the playful party crowns will make each guest feel included in the whimsical spirit.

STYLING ELEMENTS

Blue silk table cover

Blue cotton napkins

White cotton napkins
(used as a placemat)

White small plates
(salad plate or dessert
plate)

Antique silverware

Water glasses

Small vintage dishes

Cake stand

Felt crowns

Vintage trophy cup

Flowers, dried

Start with a fully draped silk table cover, created by sewing two silk fabric panels together lengthwise. The material I used is dyed a french-blue hue using natural dye from Peruvian purple corn. The color palette of soft creamy whites and earthy blues is repeated throughout the table to create a harmonious rhythm among the colors.

The placemats shown here are fashioned from large white dinner napkins. The extra layer of fabric adds texture and color while serving the practical purpose of protecting the silk table cover. If you are setting the table for children, you can keep the dinnerware and flatware simple: A salad or dessert plate along with a petite vintage fork and spoon are all that's needed when serving little ones. When serving adults, switch your plate to a dinner plate and select flatware appropriate to your meal.

The decorative felt crowns and fanciful pom-poms are an integral part of this table design, encouraging your guests to embrace their inner child. The felt crowns are loosely tied around the neatly folded napkins that top each plate. The blue silk ribbon on each crown drapes down the table, adding color and silkiness that draw you in.

A centerpiece of dried flowers adds a natural touch to this festive presentation. In this arrangement, I used dried delphinium, which perfectly complements the muted blue palette, along with dried white floral buttons, baby's breath, and everlasting flowers. Though the centerpiece is small, the contrast of the shiny, weighted, vintage trophy cup gives it a grander feel. No matter the occasion, each of your crowned guests will feel celebrated when seated at your fun and fanciful table.

above Save time the day of by making desserts and freezing them ahead of time. Many frozen treats can be kept in the freezer for up to one week. Before serving your main meal, remove your frozen desserts from the freezer, and they will be at the perfect temperature by dessert time.

above Search flea markets and antique stores for unique cups and bowls for holding little treats. Use vintage silver or glass to add a visual texture, or colored stoneware to complement your color palette.

bottom left Top dried flower stems with miniature pom-poms for a fun addition to your centerpiece arrangement. Simply snip off the flower head and use craft glue or a glue gun to attach your pom-pom to the floral stem.

FELT CROWN

When my girls were younger, I loved making wool felt crowns using naturally dyed materials. There was something about wearing a crown that transformed their everyday play into a range of theatrical scenarios. Some of our crowns were simple, and others were more elaborate for special occasions or birthdays. This felt pattern uses a long ribbon and can be adjusted to any head size, so everyone can participate in the fun.

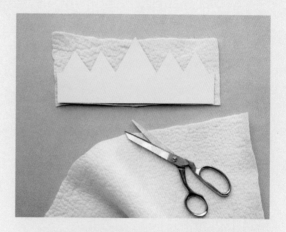

One crown

Crown template (see page 219)

8½ by 11 in [21.6 by 27.9 cm] piece of paper

Ruler

Pen or pencil

Scissors

6 by 12 in [15 by 30.5 cm] natural felt

1½ yd [137 cm] ribbon, 2 to 4 in [5 to 10 cm] in width, cut in half

3 to 4 yd [274 to 366 cm] yarn or ribbon scraps

Fabric glue or needle and thread

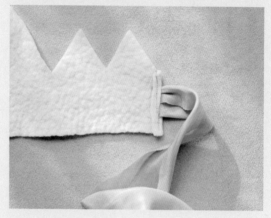

Step 1   Use the Crown Template on page 219 as a guide for your paper template. The dimensions provided outline a classic crown shape to be drawn onto an 8½ by 11 in [21.6 by 27.9 cm] sheet of paper. Start by measuring your 2 in [5 cm] band as indicated with blue lines.

Step 2   Fold the paper in half to find the center of the paper, and measure 4 in [10 cm] from the bottom of the band to create your center triangle. From there, draw two smaller triangles on each side of the center triangle to make your crown.

Step 3   With your paper folded in half, use scissors to cut out your drawn template (your folded paper will ensure your crown is symmetrical). Trace your crown template onto the felt.

Step 4   Use scissors to cut out the crown pattern on your felt. Then, cut a slit in the felt approximately 1 in [2.5 cm] long and approximately ½ in [12 mm] from each end as indicated by the gray dotted line on the template. Slide the end of one of the two ribbon pieces into the cut slit on the left side of the crown and fold the felt end over

cont'd

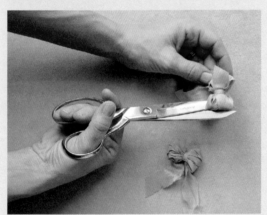

the ribbon. Sew the ends by hand or with a sewing machine to hold the ribbon in place. Repeat this process on the right side of the crown.

Step 5   Cut a 6 in [15 cm] piece of yarn or ribbon from your scraps. Set aside.

Step 6   To make a small pom-pom, wrap yarn or ribbon scraps around your index finger and middle finger twenty times, creating a series of loops. (If you have additional scraps to play with, experiment with looping the material around three fingers for a larger pom-pom.)

Step 7   Slide the loops off your fingers and use the 6 in [15 cm] piece of yarn or ribbon (set aside in step 5) to tie tightly around the center of the looped bundle, securing the pom-pom.

Step 8   Use scissors to cut open each loop—fluff to open up your pom-pom and trim to create a uniform shape.

Step 9   Attach a pom-pom to the front of your crown using fabric glue or a needle and thread.

NOTE
Make extra crowns to have on hand as birthday gifts for any age. Incorporate your crown into your birthday gift wrapping by tying the crown around your present for a festive presentation.

CELESTIAL CELEBRATION

The shimmer of crystals and the opulence of silk create an ethereal table suited for momentous occasions. A wedding, anniversary, bridal shower, milestone birthday, or New Year's Eve party is an opportunity for a monochromatic palette and showstopping hanging centerpiece.

STYLING ELEMENTS

White cotton table cover

2 off-white sheer silk table runners

White cotton napkins

White dinner plates

White pearlescent salad plates

White charger plates

Ornate sterling silver flatware

Classic water glasses

Classic wineglasses

Glass decanters, used as candleholders

Vintage glass salt dishes, used as candleholders

White beeswax taper candles

Menu 4 by 9 in [10 by 23 cm]

Crystals, geode crystals, and quartz crystals

Flowers, dried lunaria

Start your table setting with a floor-length natural white cotton table cover. Then, drape and billow silk runners across the table. Run your silk runners back and forth asymmetrically across the table; this unique placement creates movement on the table. In this presentation, I used glass decanters and vintage salt dishes as candleholders, creating a light and airy level to balance the grounding crystals.

Charger plates, also known as service plates, are traditionally used at a formal table to hold the appetizer plate and are then removed and replaced when dinner is served. Nowadays, the charger has become a decorative element on the table and can remain an accessory throughout your meal. Chargers come in various materials, such as ceramic, glass, rattan, wood, and stone, to name a few. I used a simple white charger for this design. The goal is to create height and dimension at each place setting; this brings your attention upward and adds a little distance from the waves of silk fabric on the table.

Classic white dinner plates paired with pearlescent white salad plates add luster, depth, and variety while keeping within the monochromatic theme. The contemporary dinnerware is contrasted with beautifully ornate sterling silver flatware, adding to the opulence. The napkins are pressed and folded, placed horizontally, and neatly tucked under the dinner plate. Simply placed napkins will direct your focus upward to the details of your custom menu.

Each design element is considered in this monochromatic celestial celebration. From the moment your guests are greeted by your hanging floral centerpiece, till your delectable dessert is served, a magical time will be experienced by all.

right The assorted clusters of crystals and glass decanters across the table form an asymmetrical balance that mimics the organic form of the lunaria hanging above.

Menu

Cucumber Fennel
Salad with Creamy
Herbed Dressing

Seared Scallops
& Parmesan Risotto
with Roasted
White Asparagus

White Chocolate
Mousse

left The menus are created using hand calligraphy on cardstock torn to size to create a soft deckled edging. They are then stitched to a piece of gauzy cotton fabric using a sewing machine. This simple step creates a unique custom look your guest will surely remember.

Varying the textures of your styling elements creates a monochromatic palette full of depth and tonality. Each layer engages your guest throughout the dining experience.

FLOATING FLORAL INSTALLATION
with DRIED LUNARIA

A floating floral installation instantly adds splendor to your gathering. Suspending a dried floral arrangement over your table creates an intimate space, especially when dining in a room with high ceilings. Here, I've created a dried lunaria arrangement, but feel free to experiment with other dried plants or grasses to complement your monochromatic table. Pampas grasses and baby's breath both dry to a natural white hue and are a nice alternative to lunaria. If you don't have rafters for draping your masterpiece, no worries, sturdy self-adhesive hooks will do the trick. For smaller tables or spaces, choose a shorter dowel and half the lunaria.

MATERIALS

Fishing line

¾ by 48 in [2 by 122 cm] natural wood dowel or a fallen branch

Masking tape (cream color)

20 or 30 lunaria bunches

Floral clippers

2 self-adhesive hooks

Step 1   Prepare the fishing line by measuring the distance of where you will be hanging your arrangement. Be sure to leave plenty of extra fishing line for adjusting the height. I suggest adding an additional 1 yd [1 m] when measuring. Cut two pieces of fishing line to your measured length (plus the additional 1 yd [1 m]). Tie each fishing line to the dowel, approximately 10 in [25 cm] from the end on each side. Double knot the fishing line and secure it in place with a piece of masking tape.

Step 2   Sort the lunaria bunches. Trim any damaged stems with floral clippers and sort the remaining stems into three lengths: short, medium, and long.

Step 3   Begin with the shorter stems and create small dense bunches. Secure these bunches together with the masking tape. Lunaria is very light; only a small amount of tape is needed.

Step 4   Place the short bunches horizontally against the wooden dowel, with the stems facing the center and the pods facing the ends. Attach the lunaria to the dowel with masking tape starting in the center and working outward in both directions. The goal is to camouflage the dowel. Continue to add the bunches, overlapping them slightly until you reach the end of the dowel. The last bunch of lunaria should have the stems taped to the dowel and the pods extending off the dowel.

Step 5   Next, attach the medium-length lunaria to the dowel. These can be placed as is, or if the stems are sparse, combine multiple stems with masking tape for a fuller look. Attach to the dowel as you did with the shorter stems, but tilt them upward and downward to widen the arrangement. Save a few of the medium stems for last-minute touch-ups.

cont'd

Step 6 At this point, hang the arrangement to view it in the space before finalizing it. If needed, attach the self-adhesive hooks to the ceiling for hanging, one on either side will balance the arrangement. Once the arrangement is hung, add the remaining long pieces of lunaria by simply tucking the branches into the flowers already on the dowel. You can use small pieces of tape, if necessary, to hold a stem in place, but you will likely not need tape in the final steps of adding to the arrangement.

Step 7 Use the reserved stems of lunaria from step 5 to fill in any open gaps in your arrangement. Simply tuck the remaining stems into place. Here, I've created an asymmetrical arrangement by adding more volume to the arrangement's left side, but feel free to mix it up and create a shape that inspires you.

NOTES
By using small bits of masking tape or simply tucking the light lunaria branches into place, your arrangement can be easily disassembled, and your lunaria can be repurposed for future uses. If you prefer to create a permanent arrangement, secure your lunaria branches into place with a hot glue gun.

AFTERNOON TEA

Tranquility and natural simplicity come together in a wabi-sabi-inspired table design.

STYLING ELEMENTS

Organza silk fabric

Gray cotton napkins

Earth-toned dinner plates

Black and gray ceramic bowls

Matte black flatware

Classic water glasses

Ceramic tea mugs

Brass tea strainers

Brass teapot

Ceramic candleholders

White beeswax taper candles

Four 9¾ oz [290 ml] Weck mold jars

Beauty Tea blend (see page 143)

Recipe cards

13 by 16 in [33 by 40.5 cm] gray fabric, for wrapping jar

Flowers, dried

Wabi-sabi, an ancient Japanese philosophy, celebrates nature and finding beauty in imperfections. Nature—infused into every each handcrafted detail, old and new—soothes the mind and spirit. This serene presentation, inspired by connecting with nature, is a lovely table for a quaint teatime gathering with friends.

Simple details come together eloquently in this table of understated elegance. Delicately draped silk organza panels, cut in half from a single panel, have frayed edges that add to the table's perfectly imperfect nature. The thin veil of silk offers balance and contrast to the heavy handmade ceramics on the table.

Tableware is mixed and matched, showcasing brown, black, gray, and white earthy tones. Each piece varies in texture, but the neutral hues unify them. The beauty of handmade ceramics is that each piece is completely unique.

Handmade ceramic candleholders are used to hold both beeswax candles and dried flowers. Scabiosa pods, *Astrantia*, and flax are effortlessly placed as if plucked in transition directly from the landscape. The varying textures of the candles, botanicals, ceramics, brass teapot, and fabrics encourage the eye to move through every aspect of the table. Simultaneously, the gray napkins, neatly folded in a square, create a moment of pause.

A gift of hand-blended tea is an offering to your guest and adds a design detail to each place setting. Blended loose tea is placed in glass jars wrapped furoshiki style with cotton fabric for each guest to take home and enjoy. Every table detail is thoughtfully curated yet effortlessly executed.

right Incorporate wabi-sabi into your decor using elements from nature along with vintage or handmade pieces: trimmed branches bundled in an old ceramic crock, a light pendant fashioned from a vintage wooden bowl, handmade paper pressed with dried botanicals, plaster painted walls, a reclaimed wood table, and antique wooden chairs. Each of these elements beautifully contributes to a calm and serene atmosphere.

above Handmade ceramics, crafted by artisans, are an investment meant to be loved and treasured for generations. Their balance of beauty and function make them a versatile and elegant addition to your home decor. Transform a tea mug into a vase, store precious trinkets in small bowls, and highlight collected treasures on plates or platters.

left Brass details work beautifully with natural elements, and they add warmth and color to a neutral palette.

BEAUTY TEA

Before I began growing a garden full of dye plants for color, I grew plants for herbal remedies. My dear friend and herbalist Marta and I have been friends for over a decade. We share a reverence for nature, and we love to discuss plant properties while swapping recipes we've made utilizing the plants we harvest and grow. Together, we developed Beauty Tea, created to nurture beauty inside and out. Our blend is full of antioxidants to boost immunity and fight against free radicals, nervines to calm the nervous system, and detoxifiers to release the body of toxins. We hope you enjoy a calm, radiant sense of beauty while enjoying our Beauty Tea.

Makes twenty-five to thirty servings of tea, 1 to 2 Tbsp per serving; loosely fills four 9¾ oz [290 ml] jars

INGREDIENTS

3 cups [5 g] dried calendula petals

¾ cup [12 g] dried nettles

¾ cup [6 g] dried rose petals

⅓ cup [3 g] dried chamomile flowers (whole)

¼ cup [6 g] dried oat straw

1½ Tbsp [4 g] dried elderflower

Pinch of saffron, crushed (optional)

Step 1 Place all the tea ingredients into a small bowl and toss to mix thoroughly. Store in glass jars out of direct sunlight. Herbs and flowers are photosensitive and will lose their potency if left in direct sunlight.

Step 2 To make a cup of tea, place 1 to 2 Tbsp of tea in a tea bag or mesh basket and place in a teacup. Pour 8 oz [240 ml] of almost boiling water (180°F to 190°F [82°C to 88°C]) over the tea. Cover and steep for 5 to 7 minutes or until the desired strength is reached.

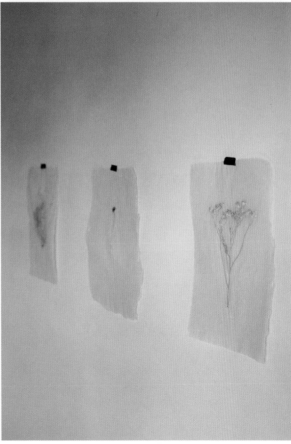

above Character and beauty are found in the impermanent and imperfect. The next time you have a vase of flowers, remove the water from your vase as the flowers start to wilt (to avoid molding) and let them dry. Find beauty in the transition from fresh to dried flowers and watch as the colors and shapes change. Dried organic roses, calendula, or chamomile flowers can be used in our tea recipe on page 143.

PLANT OASIS

*Create an intimate gathering where friends, new and old,
can connect and catch up over a casual floor-seated table
surrounded by gorgeous greenery. Pillows and pouf seating add
to the unique dining experience, encouraging guests to unwind,
relax, and revel in the company and meal to come.*

STYLING ELEMENTS

White cotton table
cover

White cotton gauzy
napkins

Assorted white plates

Speckled white
ceramic salad plates

Gray crocheted rattan
placemats

Brass flatware

Classic glassware

Earth-toned ceramic
salt dishes

White ceramic
candleholders

Glass tea light
candleholders

Beige beeswax taper
candles

Vintage and recycled
glass jars

Pillows and poufs for
floor seating

Potted plants

Flowers, dried

Incorporating houseplants and greenery is a beautiful
way to liven up your space when outdoor experiences
are limited. The varying sizes and shapes outline
your space, creating an intimate area for your
floor-seated dining. In this table, two simple coffee
tables are brought together and draped with a white
table cover. The table cover is tucked and gathered
throughout, creating a textural layer of folds, and
gauzy napkins are loosely tied around the flatware,
adding to the relaxed bohemian vibe.

The light neutral palette is a mixture of cool and
warm tones. The cool tones add a light and airy feel,
and the warm tones are calm and inviting. White
dinner plates are a mixed-and-matched assortment
of four different styles, combined with speckled
white organically shaped handmade ceramic salad
plates. While the dinner plates are assorted, having
a single line of salad plates makes the set cohesive.
The plates are placed upon cool gray placemats; the
darker hue and crocheted texture create a grounding
base, leading your eye up and across to the other
elements on the table.

Brass flatware, set upon each salad plate, adds a hint of color and unifies the tones throughout the tablescape. The glassware is simple, creating a moment of pause between the decorative elements on the table. Mini potted plants, sprigs of fern, and dried glixia flowers promenade across the table. The repeated white ceramic and glass containers create rhythm and movement, guiding you across the table.

Different tiers throughout the room keep the table warm and intimate. On the table, taper candles add height, and the contrast between the tall tapers and short tea lights keeps your eye engaged on the table. Above the table, ferns loosely hang to balance the open space. Around the table, potted plants are used to define the area, making it feel cozy while remaining open and airy.

Whether you're gathering for a special occasion or a casual evening with friends, the unique experience you compose with your floor-seated table will encourage guests to lounge, laugh, and share stories all evening long.

right The combination of dried glixia with *Pilea* plants and ferns creates a unique textural contrast that makes a lively impression.

above Mini potted *Pilea* (*Pilea peperomioides*) work as a decorative element on your table and a sweet gift for your guest to take away. Commonly known as a "money plant" or "UFO plant" for its round foliage, *Pilea* is also referred to as a "friendship plant" for its ability to easily grow and propagate, making it perfect for sharing with your friends at special gatherings like Friendsgiving.

left Place your plants on stools, benches, and shelves to create varying levels of height. To keep the space from feeling flat, avoid setting all your plants on the floor.

GLASS CONTAINER
PLANT ARRANGEMENT

Planning a pre- or post-meal activity is a great way to transition to or from your table. Setting up a planting station, where guests can create a glass container plant arrangement not only adds to your room decor but also provides a fun activity for your guests to take part in. While offering them a souvenir from a delightful evening, this simple activity allows people to have creative playtime as they chat and sip drinks before the meal or during after-dinner lingering.

For the plants, you can propagate cuttings from plants you have or purchase a selection of small plants from your local nursery. Select plants that require similar levels of light and water so that guests can mix and match in a single jar.

MATERIALS

Recycled glass jars

Pebbles

Horticultural charcoal

Potting soil

Measuring cups, or scoops

Assortment of 3 to 4 in [7.5 to 10 cm] plants or plant cuttings

Decorative moss (optional)

Step 1   Pour a base layer of pebbles, about 1 in [2.5 cm] high into a glass jar. The key to successful container planting is proper drainage.

Step 2   Add a thin layer of horticulture charcoal (used to absorb moisture odors). Follow with a layer of potting soil.

Step 3   Create a small well in the potting soil and gently nestle the plants into place, covering any roots with additional soil. Make sure the roots are surrounded by soil, not resting against the glass.

Step 4   Add decorative or live moss if you'd like to add an extra-special touch to your plant arrangement.

NOTE

Showcase your base ingredients of pebbles, charcoal, and soil in separate decorative or wood bowls.

HARVEST PALETTE

Celebrating the bounty of autumn and the shift in seasons, this Harvest Palette is inspired by the colors, flavors, and textures of fall, reminding us that beauty can be found in all cycles of transformation.

STYLING ELEMENTS

Light-gray cotton table cover

Dark-gray cotton table runner

Dusty-rose linen napkins

Earth-toned dinner plates

Earth-toned salad plates

Charcoal rattan chargers

Classic glassware

Ceramic candleholders

Natural beeswax taper candles

Mini white pumpkins

Flowers and branches, fresh and foraged

Beeswax votive candles

Grass or dried flowers

18 by 2½ in [46 by 6 cm] ribbon

Printed or handwritten name card

In the fall, the Hudson Valley, where I live, transforms into a rich earthy palette of reds, russets, and golden fall foliage. Apples, gourds, pumpkins, and chrysanthemums fill the farm stands and orchards around every corner in my town. Change is all around us, and the cooler days encourage indoor gatherings. The autumnal equinox is when the light and darkness of the day are in balance; this interplay of light and dark inspires my harvest table. I incorporate the often-overlooked lighter shades of autumn: corals, pinks, and dusty-rose hues found in the undertones of leaves and grasses, and the dark shades of gray found in the tree barks, branches, dried flowers, shrubs, and grasses remaining from summer.

The nod to light and dark starts with a light-gray table cover as the base hue. On top of the table cover, a darker charcoal-gray table runner drapes diagonally from one corner to another, in a waterfall fashion. The tonal values add depth, and the diagonal placement of the fabric and the gathering create movement as the runner cascades off the table.

Charcoal-colored rattan chargers add a layer of texture and balance to the dark table runner. Earth-toned plates add depth, warmth, and a connectedness with nature. Each plate is topped with dusty-rose napkins and a candle gift as a place card. The energy is soft and soothing, leading your eye to the bolder hues of the centerpiece.

The centerpiece is a celebration of the harvest season—a gathering of the fall landscape showcasing traditional harvest colors. Collect what you can from the wild and combine it with fall flowers and mini pumpkins available at the market or nursery. The oversized arrangement creates a grand statement as tree branches, wild bittersweet, and fall flowers overflow onto the table.

above To avoid crowding your table with an oversized centerpiece, prepare space on a side table or buffet where your centerpiece can be placed when your guests are ready to be seated. To fill the empty space, simply move your candles from the end of the table to the table's center.

As you collect natural elements for your table centerpiece, gather dried pods, leaves, and grasses to incorporate into your room decor (see Dried Botanical Wall Art on page 167). You will find an abundance of natural materials in the remains of summer and the fallen fall foliage. The kaleidoscope of hues, extracted from all facets of the autumn landscape, provides a vast palette and exudes a warm harvest welcome for all who gather.

above For an extra-special presentation, nestle a candle into each napkin as a gift for each guest. Wrap small votive beeswax candles and dried grasses with silk ribbon and print each guest's name on handmade paper, making it double as a place card.

As the days become shorter and the outside world becomes quiet, the candle is symbolic of the inner light and strength to guide us through colder days ahead.

DRIED BOTANICAL WALL ART

As an alternative to the traditional seasonal wreath, craft a botanical display that can be hung on your wall and enjoyed all year round. Creating a piece of dried botanical wall art is a wonderful way to document the season, in addition to showcasing the flowers and grasses growing in your area. You can start in the summer months by gathering a bundle of clipped flowers and grasses every few weeks. For city dwellers, save your bouquets from farmers' markets and local florists. Enjoy your blooms in a vase of water, and once they start to fade, bundle and hang your botanicals upside down to dry. Or, head outside anytime in the fall; you will find plenty of dried material to collect. Dried grasses, flowers that have faded or gone to seed, or dried leaves can all be used to create your botanical wall art. While most flowers or grass will work for drying, see my Drying Botanicals chart on page 27 for suggestions.

MATERIALS

Galvanized steel netting (see Notes, page 168)

Wire clippers

Dried botanicals

Plant clippers

Hot glue gun

Hot glue sticks

Step 1   Cut the galvanized steel netting to your desired size with the wire clippers. Here, I use an 8 by 8 in [20 by 20 cm] piece of wire netting.

Step 2   Begin with the fuller, denser dried botanicals, such as yarrow, hydrangea, or tansy.

Cut the stems to approximately 2 in [5 cm] and push them through the wire openings. Work from the center outward horizontally across the row. Once in place, hot-glue the stems to the wire.

Step 3   Continue to add the dried botanicals, row by row, alternating from top to bottom. After the first few rows are in place, you don't need to pre-trim each stem; simply add the stems through each opening until you get the placement that looks right to you and glue into place. When you have completed a few rows, you can go back and trim your stems. If needed, combine stems in a small bunch to create more bulk; this will help camouflage the wire mesh.

cont'd

Step 4 Add more botanicals and expand out from the center, and angle the flowers and grasses upward and downward to create an organic shape.

Step 5 Once the wire is filled, look for any open gaps and fill in as needed.

Step 6 Once completed, trim all excess stems from the back to ¼ to ½ in [6 to 12 mm].

NOTES

For the metal wire base, you can use galvanized steel wire netting or fencing with ½ in [6 mm] openings or any other sheet metal with openings ½ in [6 mm] or smaller. For this project, I used galvanized steel stucco netting recycled from a building project. Materials can be sourced at your local hardware store or by contacting local contractors for unusable leftovers.

Your dried botanical wall art can be created in any season. In the summer, experiment with using flowers, such as dried marigolds, globe amaranth, or strawflowers, for designing beautifully vibrant botanical wall art.

GRAZING TABLE

*An artfully curated and luxuriously laden grazing table is
perfect for both pre-dinner gatherings and as the main event.*

STYLING ELEMENTS

Light-gray cotton table
cover

White cotton table
cover

White cotton table
runner

Assorted napkins

Small plates

Vintage crocks

Small ceramic bowls

Wood bowl

Cake stands

Flat cutting boards

Footed cutting boards

Wood platter

Ceramic platter

Wood candleholders

Black beeswax taper
candles

Vases

Flowers, fresh and
dried

Adapted from a traditional buffet-style table, a
grazing table celebrates the colors and textures
of your favorite dishes and allows everyone (the
host included!) to enjoy a relaxed and stress-free
gathering. The laid-back vibe and high-impact
presentation of this table will encourage guests to
mingle while enjoying a range of delectable options.

A grazing table can be adapted to any theme or
season. The base styling elements are the same,
and the season will dictate your garnishing foods
and floral options. Gather platters, boards, bowls,
candleholders, and display stands to be used to create
varying layers of heights. Mix and match natural
materials such as wood, marble, and ceramic, but
keep the palette neutral to let the food colors shine.

To keep the foods as the main attraction, the table is
set with neutral linens as the base. A pale-gray table
cover drapes the whole table, while a white table cover,
half the length, is gathered and draped vertically. An
additional layer of a gauzy white table runner can be
gathered and tucked around the platters and boards,
creating a soft texture across the table.

One side of the table is set for self-serving. A
ceramic bowl is used to hold an assortment of cotton
napkins in light neutral hues, and the flatware is
displayed on a napkin-lined wood tray. For larger

gatherings with grazing, be sure to have ample plates for your guests, at least five more than the number of guests you expect to have. Mix and match your plates if needed; here, various small black and white ceramic plates seamlessly work together.

Fresh and dried florals are used throughout the table to add depth, texture, and color. The mix of vintage and new vases, along with the blend of soft roses and dried floral pods, creates an exciting contrast along each step of the table. Use edible flowers, plants, and herbs among the foods and on the table to add a decorative element and hint of color where needed.

above When mixing and matching plates, try to unify them by material, type, or color. Maybe your plates are assorted vintage, shades of a single color, all neutral hues, or an assortment of patterns in one color palette. When you unify them, it will look like a purposeful styling element.

Boards and platters can be assembled in the kitchen, then placed throughout the table before guests arrive. Envision your grazing table as one large cheese platter divided into many pieces that work as part of the whole. Contain your main food ingredients on your board or platter, connecting each display with nuts and fruit that overlap, intertwine, and spill over with intrigue.

Achieve balance using an assortment of textures, color, and scale when selecting your foods. Cascading grapes, vibrant fruits, artisan bread, and crackers are just a few examples of adding variety. The eye-catching arrangements you create will be a lavish feast that will delight and impress your guests.

left Stack cake stands to create a tiered display that works great as a center focal point. Floral putty can be used to secure the top stand to the bottom if you're concerned about stability.

PLATING A GRAZING PLATTER

I am never without a stash of jarred olives, nuts, spreads, ingredients for fast homemade dips, and a few boxes of crackers. With these staples on hand, I can run to the cheese shop, swing by the market for a few fruits and veggies, and be ready for guests in no time. Whether I'm hosting company or assembling a pre-dinner appetizer for my family, a grazing platter is a great presentation for snacking options.

The appeal of a grazing platter is the endless possibilities for adapting to any dietary palate. You can choose to theme your platter as savory or sweet, base it on a cuisine, or curate to a particular diet. My go-to grazing platter is cheese and charcuterie.

For family and small gatherings, I follow the formula listed in the chart on page 178 and disperse the ingredients between one to three platters or boards.

HOW TO PORTION CHEESE

Whole cheese wheels and wedges look beautiful on boards and platters, but sometimes the occasion calls for assembled platters with portioned or sliced cheeses. When serving a large group or families with younger ones, portioning and pre-slicing your cheese will keep a steady flow at your table and ease self-serving.

NOTES

When creating your grazing platter, anticipate dietary restrictions and work to include items that everyone can enjoy. For dairy-free and vegan, include a selection of vegan cheeses; for vegetarians, include ample veggies, and for gluten-free, include a selection of gluten-free crackers. Also, consider separating meats so they don't touch vegetarian or vegan items. These are just a few of the many adjustments you should be aware of when assembling your grazing table.

When designing your grazing platter, create a visual balance of colors, shapes, textures, and depth. This is easily accomplished when using an assortment of items. Fruits, berries, herbs, and nuts work wonderfully for separating similar hues. Vary your cheese cuts (cubed, sliced, wedges), and include tomatoes on the vine, vegetables, or loose capers to add a range of shapes. Artisan bread and crackers offer endless options for adding texture, and depth is achieved with small bowls, footed platters, and cascading fruits.

cont'd

INGREDIENTS

CHEESES
choose 3 types

FRESH	**SOFT**	**SEMISOFT**	**BLUE-VEINED**	**SEMIHARD**	**HARD**
Mascarpone	Brie	Fontina	Stilton	Gouda	Aged Cheddar
Ricotta	Goat	Jarlsberg	Gorgonzola	Gruyère	Parmigiano
Mozzarella	Camembert	Monterey Jack	Roquefort	Cheddar	Asiago
Feta			Danish blue	Manchego	Pecorino
Burrata			Maytag	Havarti	Romano

PANTRY ITEMS*
choose 2

Olives

Caper berries

MARINATED

Artichokes

Peppers

Tomatoes

Mushrooms

PICKLED VEGETABLES

Green beans

Peppers

Carrots

Asparagus

SWEETS
choose 3

Grapes

Figs

Pears

Pomegranates

Berries

Dried fruit*

Candied nuts*

Date loaf

Chocolate*

Preserves*

Chutney*

Honey*

DIPS AND SPREADS
choose 1 or 2

Relish*

Mustards*

Hummus

Tapenade*

Pesto*

NUTS
choose 2

Raw

Salted

Unsalted

Smoked

Seasoned

MEAT
choose 2 or
substitute vegetables

Prosciutto

Salami

Sausage

Sopressata Piccante

Speck

CRACKERS AND BREADS
choose 2 or 3

Plain crackers*

Seasoned crackers*

Seeded crackers*

Toast crackers*

Artisan bread

Gluten-free crackers*

DECORATIVE ELEMENTS

Whole fruits

Fresh mushrooms

Herbs

Edible flowers

* indicates jarred items you can keep on hand in your pantry

HOW TO PORTION CHEESE

HARD CHEESE
Shave thin slices or crumble

BLUE-VEINED CHEESE
Start at the bottom center
and fan out your cuts

SOFT WEDGE
Cut into long thin wedges

LOG
Slice across into medallions

SOFT WHEEL
Start from the center and
cut into even wedges

SEMISOFT WEDGE
Cut slices across widthwise,
then opposite across rind

STOCKED AND STYLED BAR CART

A stocked and styled bar cart adds sophistication to any event and allows you to mingle with guests, task-free while entertaining.

STYLING ELEMENTS

Cotton cocktail napkins

Styling fabric or dinner napkin

Bar towel

Glassware (assortment)

Apothecary decanters

Bar tools

Shaker glass

Ice bucket

Spirits

Mixers

Condiment dishes

Decorative bowl

Recipe books

Trays

Printable or handwritten labels

Flowers or plants

As your "cohost" for the evening, a properly assembled bar cart will offer mainstay classics along with quenching the thirst of your adventurous participants. With an assortment of handcrafted mixers, you'll take the guesswork out of assembling a crafted cocktail and encourage your guests to be creative mixologists.

Much like a table, your bar cart can be styled to suit any occasion. It showcases your cocktail options while also serving as part of your home décor. When done properly, a beautiful balance of style and function is achieved.

Your bar cart should feature all the essentials: spirits, mixers, bar tools, a shaker, an ice bucket, glasses, and cocktail napkins. No need to overfill your cart; a few premade mixers, along with three or four classic liquors, such as vodka, gin, rum, and tequila, will give your guests ample options and keep spirits high. Adding trays to your cart serves both a practical and decorative purpose. A tray on your cart's top level serves as a drink assembly area. Wood, ceramic, metal, or glass trays work well to catch drips or spills. A rattan tray on the bottom level holds mixers and additional spirits. The natural fiber, lined with a napkin or styling fabric, softens and contains your heavy glass bottles.

To balance the abundance of glass in your display, add a bowl of fruit, stack of books, candle, or plants and flowers to your cart. These items add warmth and offer the opportunity to incorporate height, texture, color, and visual contrast. Don't forget a bar towel, another useful item to add texture and color. Drape it over the handle of your bar cart, where guests can easily grab it if needed.

above When not in use for a party, your bar cart becomes a decorative display. Select a few of your favorite liquor bottles in varying shapes and heights and place them close together on a decorative tray on the top shelf, leaving enough space to display seasonal floral arrangements. Fill the middle level with an assortment of glasses and cocktail recipe books, and keep your tools and mixers on the bottom.

Decanters can be labeled with mixing instructions to guide your guest through crafting their cocktails, and herbal syrups allow for mocktails so that everyone can feel included in the festivities. Garnishes are displayed in small ceramic bowls, adding textural variety and making it easy for guests to assemble their own drinks. I recommend featuring fresh herbs, citrus wheels, and berries; they make beautiful additions to drinks and they'll add scents of herbs and citrus to your party.

top left Make cocktail recipe cards for drinks that can be created with the ingredients you have available. Print them on handmade paper and store them in a glass box or tray. Place on or near your bar cart to inspire your guests.

For gatherings where guests mingle, place small serving trays on side and end tables. This offers a resting spot for guests to set their drinks.

BOTANICAL-CRAFTED COCKTAILS

Laura Chávez Silverman is the founding naturalist of The Outside Institute, which connects people to the healing and transformative powers of nature through guided walks, workshops, and botanical mixology. Laura is inspired by the ingredients she sustainably forages in the Catskills where she resides.

Her inventive cocktails and spirit-free beverages are imbued with elusive flavors that transport you to the wild. Here, Laura shares a few of her unique botanical concoctions that use techniques of fermentation and infusion to capture the earthy spirit of the wild.

TEPACHE

Serves 6

⅓ cup [115 g] piloncillo or jaggery, or ½ cup [100 g] packed dark brown sugar

1 large organic pineapple

4 star anise pods

2 medium cinnamon sticks

2 dried chiles de árbol (optional)

Make Combine the sugar with 2 cups [480 ml] of water in a small saucepan. Set over medium-high heat and stir until the sugar dissolves. Remove from the heat and set aside to cool.

While the sugar water cools, slice off the top and bottom of the pineapple and discard. Cut away the peel and reserve the fruit for another purpose. Roughly chop the pineapple peel and place it in a gallon jar. Add the star anise, cinnamon sticks, and chiles (if using).

Pour the cooled sugar water over the pineapple peel and stir in 6 cups [1.4 L] of water. Secure a doubled piece of cheesecloth or kitchen towel over the mouth of the jar with a rubber band or string. Set the jar in a dark spot in your kitchen and allow the tepache to ferment for 2 to 3 days, or until bubbles and foam begin to form on the surface. Strain, discarding the pineapple peel and spices. Transfer the tepache to a swing-top bottle.

Tepache can be served right away, but the fullest flavor is achieved when it's fermented in the bottle at room temperature for an additional 1 to 2 days. Open the bottle daily to release any gas that builds up. Once fermentation is complete, tepache can be stored in the refrigerator for up to 1 week.

cont'd

PINEAPPLE EXPRESS COCKTAIL

Makes 1 cocktail

1 oz [30 ml] rum, tequila, or mezcal (optional)

Tepache (page 189)

1 lime wheel

1 cube crystallized ginger

Make Fill a rocks glass with ice, add the rum, then add tepache to fill. Stir, then garnish with a lime wheel and a cube of ginger.

To serve as a mocktail, pour tepache over ice in a highball glass, garnished with a lime wheel and a cube of ginger.

HERB SYRUP

Makes 1⅓ cups [320 ml]

1 cup [200 g] sugar

Handful of fresh herbs, such as thyme, rosemary, shiso, basil, lemongrass, sage, lavender, cilantro, or mint

Make In a small saucepan, heat the sugar with 1 cup [240 ml] of water until the sugar dissolves. Remove from the heat. While the mixture is still hot, stir in a large handful of fresh herbs. Cover the pan and cool completely, or steep overnight for a stronger herbal flavor. Strain and discard the herbs. Refrigerate the syrup until cold, and store in the refrigerator for up to 2 weeks.

NOTE
Extra herb syrup is delicious drizzled over fresh fruit.

THE SECRET GARDEN

Makes 1 cocktail

2 oz [60 ml] gin

1 oz [30 ml] herb syrup (recipe above)

1 oz [30 ml] fresh lime juice

Absinthe

Pinch of fennel pollen or ground fennel seeds

1 herb sprig

Make Fill a shaker with ice and add the gin, herb syrup, and lime juice. Shake vigorously and pour into a rocks glass. Mist with absinthe from a spray bottle and garnish with a pinch of fennel pollen and an herb sprig.

To serve as a mocktail, fill a rocks glass with ice, then add the herb syrup and lime juice. Fill with tonic. Stir, then garnish with a pinch of fennel pollen and an herb sprig.

NORDIC WINTER

This table is inspired by the aesthetics of Scandinavian design, which embraces a monochromatic palette, clean lines, natural textures, and earthy elements.

STYLING ELEMENTS

2 white cotton covers

White cotton table runner

White cotton napkins

Black dinner plates

Walnut wood bowls

Matte black flatware

Smoky gray vintage glasses

Birchwood candleholders with tea light candles

Black iron candleholders

White beeswax taper candles

White ceramic serving tray

Black ceramic vase

Pine branch, foraged

Fallen tree branches

Felt stars

The simplicity of form and quality of craftsmanship is seen throughout Scandinavian design. Layered linens and wood accents offer warm touches while keeping the look clean and minimal. The unencumbered openness lures you to sit, comfortable and contented, among foraged greens and a crackling fire, all evening long.

In this presentation, the cozy ambiance of layered white linens creates the neutral base of your table design. In slightly varying lengths, two white table covers drape the table, topped with a gauzy white table runner. The multiple layers create a veil of white hues on the table. The whites are contrasted with black plates and topped with hand-turned walnut bowls to soften the transition.

White cotton napkins loosely draped on each plate resemble a white pillow of snow, adding to the winterland feel. Smoky gray glasses, purchased at an antique shop, complement the color palette and add an authentic modern touch to the table. Each place setting is completed with clean and contemporary matte black flatware framing each setting.

The key is to create a feeling of simplicity without letting the table feel flat. Scale, color, and form are used to create depth and keep the eye engaged. The

large tree branch, a bowl of clementines, birch log candleholders, and cast-iron candlesticks guide your eye across the table. The asymmetrical balance is peaceful and engaging.

When selecting design elements for your table, consider each shape and how it will contribute to the overall look of the table. Similar forms create a pattern and a sense of order. These simple, thoughtful touches create a warm and welcoming table, perfect for a cozy winter evening.

right On winter walks, keep your eyes open for moss, pods, twigs, nuts, or pine cones to collect and display in wooden bowls as wintertime decor. Use fallen branches, cedar, pine, juniper, fir, holly, or any winterberry as a single stem in a vase or displayed in a large oversized arrangement.

above Use leftover wool felt from your crown-making project on page 121 to make little star ornaments. Simply cut out two stars and glue them together, securing twine or thin wire in the center for hanging.

left The soft glow of candles adds warmth to the room. A hanging wreath of foraged greens and candles adds a magical touch to the air that will transport you to simpler times. Nothing is more enchanting than dining by candle- and firelight, cozied up to the table with family and friends.

HOLIDAY GIFT WRAPPING

Create memories and new traditions with the after-dinner activity of holiday gift wrapping. A beautifully stocked gift wrapping station will add to the cozy and festive ambience of your winter gathering. Have guests bring their boxed gifts to be wrapped, and enjoy an evening full of fun and nature-inspired wrapping.

Scandinavian-style gift wrapping often features earthy, brown paper packages wrapped in string and twine. While I love the natural feel of brown kraft paper, I find it festive to use gold and black wrapping paper for holiday gifting. A matte gold paper has the same earthy feel as kraft paper, but the gold shimmer adds an extra special touch. Matte black wrapping paper is an unexpected option for holiday gifting, but it's my go-to for any occasion; it adds mystery and makes your natural ribbon colors and earthy elements pop.

MATERIALS

Assortment of wrapping paper

Plant-dyed ribbons

Name tags

Embellishments: berry branches, winter greens, brass bells, felt stars

Scissors

Tape

Tissue paper

Step 1   Designate an area for gift wrapping. It can simply be floor seating around a coffee table, a folding table designated for your activity, or the dinner table once your meal is cleared.

Step 2   Lay out an assortment of wrapping paper, ribbons, name tags, and embellishments for your guests to choose from. Embellishments can be sorted in decorative bowls to create a beautiful display.

Step 3   Wrap a few boxes with wrapping paper (these can be empty), tie with a ribbon, and tuck in or tie a decorative embellishment on top. These samples will guide and inspire your guests when doing their own gift wrapping.

NOTE

Add the holiday scent of cloves to your space by making orange pomanders. Simply poke cloves into your oranges in any pattern and place them in a ceramic or wooden bowl. The spicy-citrusy scent will fill your room for days.

Displaying a collection of white pillar candles in varying heights is an easy and impactful way to dress up tables and other surfaces in your home. I keep three of each in the following heights, 3, 6, 8, and 10 in [7.5, 15, 20, and 25 cm], and I use them in various combinations. To decorate your fireplace mantel, clip some fresh greens from outdoors and add them among your white pillar candles.

BREAKFAST IN BED

Breakfast in bed is a wonderful way to embark upon a celebra-tory day—Mother's Day, Father's Day, an anniversary—or provide a mindful moment of pause before easing into the day. Whether you are treating a loved one or yourself, taking a bit of time to enjoy the luxury of a warm, nourishing breakfast in the comfort of bed brings a sense of peace and indulgence to start your day.

STYLING ELEMENTS

Charcoal cotton table cover (headboard)

White cotton table cover (curtains)

Light-gray cotton styling fabric (nightstand)

Rose cotton napkins

Mauve cotton styling fabric (tray)

Rattan serving tray

Avocado-dyed silk pillowcases (see page 83, optional)

Hand-knit wool blanket (see page 208, optional)

The bedroom is your sanctuary. While you don't need to redecorate to accomplish a cozy morning in bed, consider how naturally dyed textiles can add to the ambience in the room.

The light and airy curtains, the grounding feel of the fabric-draped headboard, and the inviting bed coverlet are all ways to utilize textiles to create a soft, calm, and serene space.

Textiles play an integral role in your bedroom decor; cotton, linen, wool, and silk—each material offers contast and character to the room. The curtains, headboard, side table, bed, and floor are all opportunities to use textural elements to soften your space. Overlapping colors and textures create a sense of depth and add coziness to the room. Shades of blue-gray bed linens add a calming, relaxed feel, while the contrast of the light, blush-pink pillowcases add a bit of liveliness.

Incorporate living elements of nature into your bedroom. Plants and flowers can balance your overall design, and a few houseplants mixed with seasonal blooms offer textural contrast and seasonal scents. In this presentation, I used a dark woodsy quince branch with pink petal blossoms to add to the nature-inspired palette.

Adding seasonal flowers or forcing flowering branches indoors during the colder months brings life and color to your home decor. The process of "forcing" flowering branches refers to pruning outdoor flowering trees and shrubs that bloom in the spring and bringing them indoors in late winter. The warmer indoor temperature will force open the flowering blooms so they can be enjoyed months earlier. Some of my favorites are apple, cherry, forsythia, magnolia, pussy willow, and quince. Bringing a few stems indoors is all that's needed to make the space feel warm and inviting.

above For my knitting friends, my mom has shared her pattern for my bedroom throw blanket. Knit throw pattern: 36 in circular needle, size 17 [91 cm, 12.75 mm]. Use 10 skeins of 100 percent merino chunky yarn 4 oz [approximately 55 yd] (yarn from Camellia Fiber Company). Seed stitch: Knit 1, purl 1 across row. Next row: Purl the knit stitch, knit the purl stitch. Cast on 70 stitches. Knit 3 rows for the border. Next, knit 3 stitches, seed stitch to last 3, then knit 3. Continue to length. Knit 3 rows, then cast off stitches.

above To create the Breakfast in Bed tray, follow the same formula as the bedroom decor by including layers of linens, textural contrast, and a bit of nature. For my tray, I used a warm rosy napkin to line a dark rattan tray, and a lighter shade of napkin to roll the flatware tightly. There is no style or color guide for the cups and plates for serving; choose what you love and be sure to select pieces that are sturdy and weighted to avoid spillages on the way to or in bed. Complete the tray with a small bunch of fresh flowers, a savory dish, and a hot cup of coffee, and you've planted the seed for a perfect day ahead.

SAVORY BREAKFAST BOWL

Enjoying the leisurely act of breakfast in bed every so often is a simple luxury we all should indulge in. Taking a slower approach to your morning can help soothe the mind and body, and set the tone for the day ahead. Enjoy this savory breakfast bowl in a quiet, comfortable space, soaking in a moment of calm before entering the activities of the day.

This Savory Breakfast Bowl was inspired by the staples I keep on hand in my kitchen, but feel free to change it up with your choice of veggies. I like to mix in salsa and a dollop of sour cream for extra hits of flavor.

Serves 2

INGREDIENTS

½ lb [230 g] baby potatoes

Salt

Olive oil

1 pint cherry tomatoes

Black pepper

1 garlic clove, finely chopped

¼ cup [5 oz] baby spinach

1 or 2 green onions, white parts chopped

3 eggs

1 ripe avocado

Chives (optional, for garnish)

Step 1   Place the potatoes in a saucepan or pot and cover with 1 to 2 in [2.5 to 5 cm] of cold water and add a pinch of salt. Bring to a boil and then lower the heat to a simmer. Cook uncovered for 5 minutes or until tender. Drain and set aside.

Step 2   In a sauté pan, heat 1 Tbsp of olive oil over medium heat. Add the tomatoes to the pan, turn the heat to low, and cook for 5 to 7 minutes, or until the skins burst and the bottoms slightly blacken. Season with salt and pepper, remove from pan, and set aside.

Step 3   Add 2 Tbsp of olive oil to the sauté pan and add the cooked potatoes. Sauté over medium heat till browned. Once the potatoes are browned, move them to one side of the pan, add ½ Tbsp of olive oil and the chopped garlic to the clear side of the pan, and sauté for 30 seconds. Then add the spinach and a splash of water and toss with the garlic. Turn the heat to low and allow the spinach to wilt. Remove from the pan and set aside.

Step 4   Heat ½ Tbsp of olive oil in the sauté pan over medium heat. Add the chopped green onions and sauté for 1 to 2 minutes. Whisk the eggs with 1 Tbsp of water and add to the pan. Scramble the eggs to your taste.

Step 5   Divide the ingredients between two bowls and drizzle with olive oil. Season with salt and pepper, add half the avocado, and garnish with chives, if desired.

right My soft pink-blush pillow-cases and sheet are dyed with avocado pits. Create your own avocado-dyed pillowcase using my Avocado-Dyed Napkins how-to on page 83. For one silk or cotton pillowcase, start with 5 to 10 avocado pits (the more pits you use, the darker the color you will achieve).

RESOURCES

To help you get started, here are sources for the items in my home collection and displayed in this book. Antique stores and flea markets are also go-tos; I encourage you to explore your local offerings. Have fun creating!

Table Linens
Silk & Willow | *silkandwillow.com*

Tableware
Anthropologie | *anthropologie.com*
CB2 | *cb2.com*
Crate & Barrel | *crateandbarrel.com*
IKEA | *ikea.com*
Pottery Barn | *potterybarn.com*
Restoration Hardware | *rh.com*
West Elm | *westelm.com*
William Sonoma | *williams-sonoma.com*

Handmade Ceramics
1220° Ceramics | *1220ceramics.com*
Convivial | *convivialproduction.com*
Food52 | *food52.com*
GG05DesignLedStudio | *etsy.com/uk/shop/GG05DesignLedStudio*
gritCERAMICS | *gritceramics.com*
Handmade Studio TN | *handmadestudiotn.com*
Julie Hadley | *juliehadley.com*
Kabinshop | *kabinshop.com*
Laima Ceramics | *laimaceramics.com*
Millet & Hammer | *milletandhammer.com*
Notary Ceramics | *notaryceramics.com*
Rebecca Williams Ceramics | *rebeccawilliamsceramics.co.uk*
Silk & Willow | *silkandwillow.com*
Tagliaferro Ceramics | *tagceramics.com*
Tellefsen Atelier | *tellefsenatelier.com*
Trace Aesthetic | *traceaesthetic.myshopify.com*
Young Earth Ceramics | *etsy.com/shop/YoungEarthCeramics*

Tables and Furniture
Crate and Barrel | *crateandbarrel.com*
IKEA | *ikea.com*
Pottery Barn | *potterybarn.com*
Restoration Hardware | *rh.com*
Sawkille Co. | *sawkille.com*
West Elm | *westelm.com*
Williams Sonoma | *williams-sonoma.com*

Calligraphy
House of Modern Letters | *houseofmodernletters.com*
Rare Bird Font Foundry | *rarebirdfonts.com*
Seniman Calligraphy | *senimancalligraphy.com*
Written Word Calligraphy | *writtenwordcalligraphy.com*

Handmade Paper and Plant-Dyed Ribbon
Silk & Willow | *silkandwillow.com*

Sustainable Fabrics
Aurora Silk | *aurorasilk.com*
Maiwa | *maiwa.com*
Mood Fabrics | *moodfabrics.com*
Silk & Willow | *silkandwillow.com*

Event Spaces
Afternoon Tea and Botanical Birthday
The Dutchess | *thedutchess.com*

Weekend Brunch, Date Night In, Garden Gathering, Modern Dutch Master
Foxfire Mountain House | *foxfiremountainhouse.com*

Celestial Celebration, Ocean Inspired
Audrey's Farmhouse | *audreysfarmhouse.com*

MENU TEMPLATE *see page 95*

CARDSTOCK MENU
3½ by 5 in [9 by 12 cm]

HANDMADE PAPER "FOLDER"
7½ by 5½ in [19 by 12 cm]

SCALE 100%

CROWN TEMPLATE *see page 121*

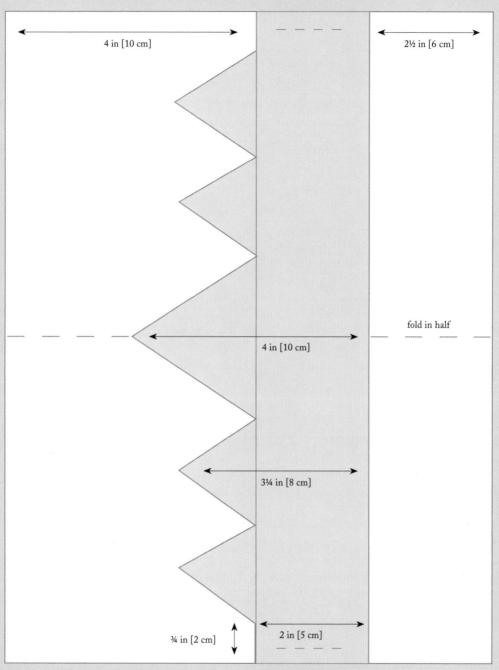

4 in [10 cm]

2½ in [6 cm]

fold in half

4 in [10 cm]

3¼ in [8 cm]

¾ in [2 cm]

2 in [5 cm]

SHEET OF PAPER

8½ by 11 in [21.6 by 27.9 cm]

NOT TO SCALE

ACKNOWLEDGMENTS

My family is the driving force behind every project I undertake. Without their inspiration, support, and encouragement, I could not have embarked on the adventurous path of following my dreams and starting a business based on my environmental values and passion for creating.

Jay, the universe destined us to be together for a reason, and I would be lost without you. Thank you for our twenty-five-plus-year partnership that grows stronger with every passing year. For taking the leap to leave your job to support my dream of a business we can build together; you bring the perfect balance to my chaotic creative journey.

To my "chickens," Catherine and Elizabeth, from the moment you were born, you guided me on the path to a cleaner, nature-focused life. Picturing your little faces and the joy and wonder you found in the simplicity of nature inspires me every day. Thank you for being my playmates and my excuse to be a kid as we played and explored the world around us. You both continue to amaze me daily with the creative, bright, caring, beautiful humans you are today.

To my parents, John and Andrea, your lives of service and tending to others' needs left a lasting impression. We are blessed to be recipients of your selfless giving and unwavering support. Mom, thank you for never turning down a knitting project, even when most of my ideas don't have a pattern. Your knitted throw blanket, knitted pillow, and pouf covers added a special touch to the book (Plant Oasis and Breakfast in Bed). Aunt Johanne, thank you for being my gardening expert and for the countless hours of planting, pruning, clipping, hanging, and drying flowers throughout the summer months. Thank you for your willingness to take on new crochet projects; your crochet placemats are a favorite and were perfect for my Plant Oasis table.

Mimi, your creativity and artistry has been an inspiration for as long as I can remember (since I met Jay when I was fifteen years old). You are the queen of gift wrapping, over-the-top birthday celebrations, extravagant holiday table decorating, and twig collecting (or anything else interesting you find on your morning walks). You were the first to jump in and encourage me to share my story. Our brainstorming and notecard-making sessions were so much fun; you were the push that put it all into motion.

Corbin, I can't thank you enough for taking on this creative endeavor with me. Without you, this book would not have been the same. You brought vibrancy and life to each image. I learned so much from watching you work. Your professionalism and unique eye for capturing each detail is truly remarkable. My gratitude is beyond words.

To my agents, Leslie Stoker and Leslie Jonath, thank you for your belief in my art and for having faith in the ideas I wanted to share. Chronicle Books, it's such a thrill to be a part of your community; I'm honored to have earned your trust. To my editor, Rachel Hiles, thank you for your calm and caring demeanor and for creating the vision that made this book a reality.

To Eliza Clark and Tim Trojian of Foxfire Mountain House (Weekend Brunch Table, Date Night In, Garden Gathering, Modern Dutch Master), Rameet Chawla and Shibani Clews of The Dutchess (Afternoon Tea, Botanical Birthday), and Sally Watkinson and Doug Posey of Audrey's Farmhouse (Celestial Celebration, Ocean Inspired), thank you for your immense generosity and for opening your beautiful spaces and allowing me to create in them. Each space is so special and unique, bringing ambiance and life to each table.

Kiana Underwood, thank you for your friendship and flower-creating genius. It was such a treat to work with you and have you be a part of my book; my Modern Dutch Master would not have been the same without your extraordinary floral masterpiece. Jonah Meyer and Tara DeLisio of Sawkille Co., thank you for your exquisite craftsmanship, adding the perfect detail to my Nordic Winter table with your handcrafted wood bench and stool. Laura Chávez Silverman, of The Outside Institute, thank you for your botanical expertise and contribution to my Stocked and Styled Bar Cart with your creative concoctions. Tim Trojian, of Foxfire Mountain House, thank you for creating your delectable galette for my Weekend Brunch table and for sharing the recipe for everyone to enjoy. Silbia Ro, thank you for your exquisite calligraphy sprinkled throughout the book and for your illustrations that explain the process of styling and sizing table linens. Alexis Tellefsen, your treasured pieces, used throughout this book, are heirlooms I will forever cherish. Thank you for sharing your craft with me! Marta Porras, your connection to the plant world is magical. Thank you for your input and expertise on my Beauty Tea recipe. Your thoughtful care and consideration for each ingredient made it extra special.

Carol, my dearest friend for more than thirty-five years, you have been there for everything! And once again, you offer your open and continued support with my book-writing endeavor. Thank you for always being there to bounce ideas around and for helping me to find clarity in my rambling thoughts and ideas. Johnine, I'm lucky to have you as my sister. You inspire me with your fierce loyalty and commitment to your beliefs. Thank you for your support and for cheering me along in my journey. To my family and friends not listed, I see and feel your encouragement in the many ways you offer it; thank you.

Last, to my Silk & Willow community, you're the best! I am inspired and driven by the creative ways you use our linens and ribbons. The stories and notes you've shared, of incorporating our textiles into your momentous life events, hold a special place in my heart. With my warmest gratitude, thank you!